GHOST TOWNS

and Historical Haunts in

ARIZONA

Stories and Photos by

Thelma Heatwole

GOLDEN WEST ☼
PUBLISHERS

Front cover photo—Miner's shack crumbling away at Tip Top.

Back cover photo—Desert artifacts mark garden museum at Conde home.

Physical hazards may be encountered in visiting ghost towns, particularly old mining localities. Land ownerships and road conditions change over the years. Readers should take proper precautions and make local inquiries, as author and publishers cannot accept responsibility for such matters.

Library of Congress Cataloging in Publication Data

Heatwole, Thelma
    Ghost towns and historical haunts in Arizona.

    "Articles which have appeared in the Arizona republic."
    Includes index.
    1. Cities and towns, Ruined, extinct, etc.--
Arizona--Guide-books. 2. Arizona--Description and travel--1951-   --Guide-books. I. Title.
F809.3.H4   979.1   80-26433
ISBN 0-914846-10-8

Printed in the United States of America

Golden West Publishers
4113 N. Longview Ave.
Phoenix, AZ. 85014, USA

*This book is dedicated
to my thoughtful husband
Don.
His untiring help and support
made possible the pursuit
of ghost towns, historical haunts
and backwoods stories.*

PRECAUTIONS

Ghost town visitors must be cautious.

Many areas are pocked with mines, pot holes, old wells. People have met their death by falling into such places.

Don't forget the desert washes that flood and the quicksand that may lurk in riverbeds, streams and water holes.

Be sure your vehicle can travel the terrain successfully. Even then, be careful. We suffered two ruptured gas tanks in our four-wheel drive vehicle.

Gas, food, water and first aid supplies must be sufficient. We ran out of gas once. It was no fun and caused delay, stress and trouble.

Keep an eye out for snakes and other denizens of the remote country. Know the vegetation.

Observe "no trespassing" and "keep out" signs.

Don't get lost. Tell a friend or family member where you are going, and about when you will return. Know desert survival. Our vehicle is equipped with citizen band radio—for emergencies.

Commonwealth Hill—its riches launched Pearce.

CONTENTS

Forlorn, abandoned entranceway to early-day Gleeson schoolhouse

SETTING THE STAGE
for Arizona adventures

Ghost towns—sagging tributes to pioneering forefathers—live on in Arizona. Some boast sizable remnants. Others have all but vanished.

Some fragmented remains huddle eerily in ragged clusters in the desert and hills. Other historical haunts are hard to find. The pursuit of a ghost town can be likened to hunting for a buried treasure—the very illusiveness provides added elixir.

Once we hunted all afternoon for a ghost town in the Bradshaws, traipsing hills and bottomlands without success. Lunch time came and went. The sun waned. In a last ditch effort, my husband Don climbed a mountain to scan the terrain with binoculars. He shouted when he spied part of a rock structure in an area that somehow had escaped us. Reaching the old mining camp, our paydirt came in witnessing a piece of history.

I shall never forget ghost town Swansea, where we found graves had been removed from the old cemetery—leaving rows of tell-tale rectangular gaps. We learned later from a state office that it was indeed the work of ghouls. The mystery comprised a separate story in time for the *Arizona Republic* on Halloween.

Such episodes help explain the motivation behind ghost town expeditions. For those who love Arizona outdoors, hunting ghost towns with pedigree pasts is stimulating and adventuresome.

Don Bufkin, assistant to the director of the Arizona Historical Society, says there are more than 500 definable "ghost town" places in Arizona, depending on the specific definition of a ghost town.

Unfortunately, he said most Arizona ghost towns today exist only in the dusty files of long gone newspapers, memories of old time residents, postal records, old time maps or other documentary sources.

The Arizona ghost town that can still boast a collection of abandoned but still standing structures is a rare collection. Bufkin said, "It's the rarity of the ruins and the problems connected with finding the 'lost' places that add fascination to the quest."

Hence, this book's ghostly places with tangible relics has merit. Stories in this book are largely as they appeared under my byline in *The Arizona Republic.*

Now, why did I write all the ghost town stories? They reflect a personal quest and interest which, it developed, were in tune with many readers. During my 16 years as a full time staffer for *The Arizona Republic* with a beat of eight valley cities, I also explored ghost towns in many regions of the state. The quest was insatiable.

One ghost town simply whetted the appetite for another. Since retirement from my news beat, I have continued ghost town travel.

It seemed fitting that the travel stories over many years be packaged for fans of Arizona backwoods places. Study and reflection on places and history help today's generation appreciate the present and respect the future.

This book is not simply to repeat bits of history, but to whet interest in Arizona haunting places.

Sifting legend from fact is difficult. Interspersed in these accounts is historical information—some probably legendary, some gleaned from people who lived in the heyday of the towns.

Old files at the *Arizona Republic* were helpful. *Arizona Place Names* and the Arizona Historical Society in Tucson were good sources of reference.

While history, then, is a strong thread in this book, it is only one ingredient. The main theme chronicled here is the outdoor adventure in visiting historical haunts, and the vibes that may be encountered. The words and pictures depict what today's fans may encounter at the sites.

A special page is devoted to precautions. One that deserves repetition is: Stay away from mines and nearby areas. These places are dangerous. Avoid them like a plague.

Most towns reflect a desertion prompted usually when the mines played out. A few like Agua Caliente—which existed for a different purpose, and Cleator—have fragile hold on existence today. Each has a souvenir past. Oatman is not a ghost town per se, but as one resident said, "We like to be considered the liveliest ghost town in

On the road to Hualapai "mansion"

Adobe walls peek through old trees at Charleston.

Arizona." Because of the town's innate character, it is included in this book.

My husband made the pursuit of ghost towns possible. On many trips our helpful companions were John and Winifred Lynch, whose interest in ghost towns matched ours. At least twice, we would have abandoned searches had it not been for John's perseverance.

Charleston is memorable. We had all but given up hope of finding the ghost town when Lynch waded across the San Pedro River. Scouting ahead, he spotted an adobe structure through a tangle of mesquite. He hollered for us to follow. It was bitter cold that first day of January. We learned later that the day set a record.

The only way I could wade and save my panty hose was to take them off. I stepped behind the Jeep, hoping no train would zip along the nearby railroad track and pulled off the hose—a breezy process. I put my slacks back on, summoned courage and inched across the river to avoid pitfalls—the wind blowing like mad.

Once across, I stepped sandy feet into shoes and readied my camera for action. It was late afternoon. Shadows were lengthening, casting uncanny forms. Old trees had jungled in the years since the town's demise. There was a maze of little paths among the old adobes.

The whole venture, though, was a dish I love. I wrote at the scene with hands so cold they would hardly manipulate: "Charleston is a bonanza in adobe, crumbling into decaying weird foundations. There must be no equal to this ghost town."

Dos Cabezas in southern Arizona was unforgettable. It was wintertime and we arrived well after dark at a motel reserved for us in Willcox. Local businessman Johnny Hidalgo, by previous arrangement, met with us to give valuable information about the area.

So much occurred in Dos Cabezas' past. Feature: a stage coach stop with a gunsight hole in the wall for firearms. Residents were friendly, providing much information. The place called for a repeat visit years later.

The old hotel in Agua Caliente was fascinating. An old man looking after the otherwise unused building said he was out of food. He persuaded my husband (while I was working at the scene) to take him to Hyder, about seven miles away. My husband complied, but was chagrined when the man came out of the store—not with food— but six quarts of wine.

The fun and excitement of quests for Arizona ghost towns live on. In a memory montage there were:

—The day the old man of the desert near Sasco told us how to brew sagebrush tea; the thrill of staying in ancient Morenci Hotel where steam pipes crackled in the night, startling us in our bed.

—The time we accidentally ran into a burro hunting party in the Bill Williams River area; the day we learned there really is a way to Paradise—right here on earth—an Arizona ghost town, in fact.

—Times when I fell, receiving scratches and bruises but always managing to protect my camera; the flat tires in faraway places; the quiet restful nights in Lookout Motel, Tombstone, overlooking the purple-hued hills steeped with history. The past is easy to recall in fancy in that colorful country.

—At Fort Misery—there was the satisfaction after a long hunt when the grave of "Old Kentuck," smothered in weeds, was finally located. "If only Old Kentuck could know how gratifying it was to find this tombstone," I said. Someone else in the party observed, "Maybe he does."

And, then, there was the time one 20-gallon gas tank (our Jeep Wagoneer is equipped with two tanks) proved empty when we thought one was full. Another time, we ran out of gas at Sunflower at twilight—it seems often the trauma things happen about that time. There were no gasoline facilities.

Just when we were wondering if we were destined to spend the

Old adobe etched with gun well at Dos Cabezas

First frame house in Paradise stands eroded and gaunt

night in the car, we received an offer, from an officer, of five gallons of gas if we would transport a stranded woman to Phoenix. We did —with some trepidation.

Once, too, we sprang a leak in our gasoline tank and the gas poured out as though coming from some fountain. We were in a remote area of the Galiuro Mountains but, fortunately, the extra gas tank saved us.

Car trouble high in the Chiricahua Mountains almost spelled disaster, but somehow the Jeep limped out and kept going until, on a dusty backroad ten miles from Tombstone, it conked out, completely.

Again, we considered food supplies and a possible night out. We try always to travel with another couple—there's safety in numbers. This time, luck was with us. A telephone company truck came along with two helpful young men. They tried unsuccessfully to get the car going, then radioed in for a wrecker. Our Good Samaritan almost blew his good deed when he advised the radio home base that "four elderly people" were stranded. We laughed at the reference.

The telephone truck drove on, disappearing in the distance and we awaited the tow truck arrival. It was the first time I ever backed into Tombstone.

Hopefully, this book reflects the fascination of pursuing Arizona's lesser known but legendary places. Ghost town hunters will develop their own set of unexpected encounters in the process. My earnest hope is that the only thing fans take at the scene are pictures—tailored for cherished memories.

Visiting ghost towns involves precautions that must be observed. Please keep them in mind as you enjoy your adventures in Arizona's past.

Happy haunting!

GRIM REMINDERS
the hazard of old mine shafts

A walk in the desert-pretty Hieroglyphic Mountains east of Morristown recently came to a shuddering halt with the sight of several open mine shafts yawning in great depth without fencing, covering or posting.

Couples camped in the general area kept dogs tied or confined in their trailer home. They said their pets could chase a rabbit and fall in the depths and never be retrieved.

Far worse—children and adults can and have tumbled to their deaths in such shafts. Old mines also have been used for disposal of dead bodies.

This particular site is in lush mountain and desert country, an area frequented by Sun Citians and rockhounds who camp overnight in the hills. Old foundations indicate former mining activity, reportedly for gold.

Newspapers occasionally report deaths of people falling into old mines. The hazardous shafts are located throughout the state—on state and national forest land and in Bureau of Land Management territory.

News files reveal an instance where an 8-year-old boy slid from his father's motorcycle 165 feet to his death down an abandoned mine shaft. His parents were awarded $135,000 in judgment against the National Park Service.

In 1977, a 36-year-old man dropped 145 feet to his death in a weed-covered abandoned mine shaft after he stepped out of his car beside the road near Tombstone. And, in 1975, a 20-year-old man tumbled 100 feet down a deserted shaft near Wickenburg and died.

Chuck Titus, of the Arizona Mine Inspector office, said the state is "peppered" with such mine shafts. It is difficult to identify owners.

"At one time in this state these open shafts were an issue during an election. One candidate said he was going out and fill all of them. But, I don't know how he was going to do it. They are spread out all over the state," Titus said.

Titus asked this reporter to send in the location of the mines in the Hieroglyphic Mountains so that the information would be given to a mine inspector deputy.

The law says that owners are liable to keep all abandoned shafts and prospect holes covered, posted and fenced in, Titus said.

"We welcome reports of open abandoned mine shafts. We send a deputy out, investigate, try to identify the owner and get them to properly post, cover and protect it. If not, we put up a danger sign. That's all we are permitted to do by law," Titus said.

"We appreciate these notifications from the general public so we can do what we can under the law to protect the public," he added.

An old mine shaft gapes not far from roadway to old town.

WESTERN

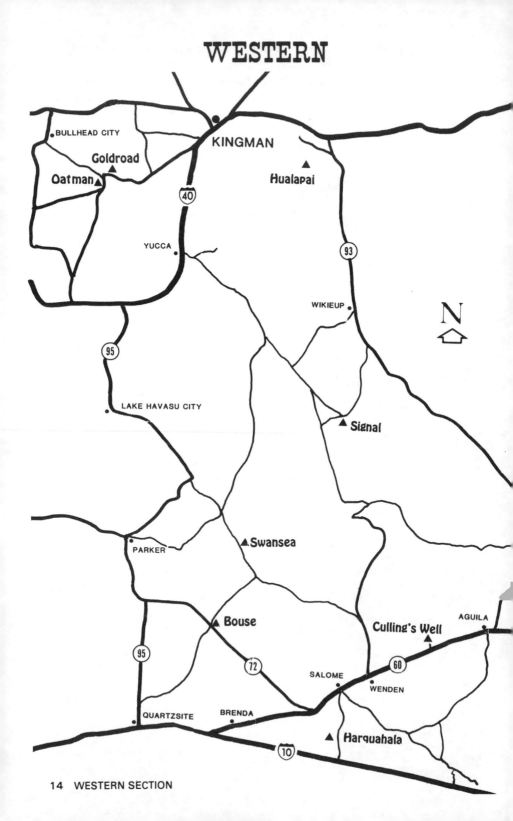

BOUSE
museum of the past

R.L. Lyman, a former school teacher, devotes his energy and time to recapturing and preserving history in this remote setting along state Route 72 enroute to Parker.

Ten years ago he bought land on the edge of Bouse and established his Black Mountain Trading Post and Museum.

Since then he has been restoring old buildings, some already on the property or brought in from Bouse, including the old jail, the Brayton Saloon, a blacksmith shop and a store.

Those who savor things historical and like to prowl among artifacts will relish the museum. Altogether some 3,500 items fill the place. A moonshine still labeled "used in the late 1800s in the hills of Globe," a huge collection of model railroad cars dating from 1888 and the old Brayton Post Office are some examples.

There is a room of antiques, collectibles and junk such as license plates, Prince Albert tobacco cans, bottles galore, books and carnival glass. Some items are for sale.

Outdoors are old automobiles, a trolley car and a replica being rebuilt of a 120-year-old engine, "The General of Civil War Fame."

15

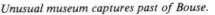

Unusual museum captures past of Bouse.

Bouse museum owner R. L. Lyman fashions metal monsters.

Lyman said rebuilding started 40 years ago.

Bouse, once busy with mining-related activities and as a rail tangent for mines at Swansea (now a ghost town 30 miles away), was originally called Brayton. It was named for John Brayton Martin, who operated the Brayton Commercial Co.

The name was changed in 1907 to Bouse, but there is a question whether it was named for a miner and truck gardener or for a trader and storekeeper. Both were named Bouse.

Mining operations have ended, but history, through Lyman's effort is the attraction. He is trying to re-create the town as it was earlier in the century.

Admission fees—$1 adults, 50 cents children—go to pay yearly taxes.

His museum includes many of his paintings in oil and watercolor, but he also has interesting works in tin and copper and some rock paintings. He also makes metal "monsters."

Lyman places big emphasis on Indian lore. "I bought the place when I found that it was an old Indian town." He has discovered numerous Indian relics on the property.

The museum, just south of still-active Bouse, is open from 8 a.m. to 5 p.m. seven days a week.

CULLING'S WELL
the lighthouse on the desert

In its time, Culling's Well was a lifesaver, but searching for the former "lighthouse of the desert" station is difficult.

The well was the only stable source of water between Wickenburg and Ehrenberg.

A lamp suspended at the top of a pole was a beacon to travelers lost at night in the wilderness—hence the "lighthouse" name.

Today the buildings that surrounded it have been claimed by the desert or removed. Gone are the adobe walls of the old station house, replaced by a timeworn tree, a few old nails, shards of glass and piles of rocks.

A cracked water trough, probably built in later years, is invaded by desert shrubs. The well is still there but dry and partially filled.

The well was built more than a century ago by Charles C. Culling, whom friends described as a "good, whole-souled, jovial man, always giving a hearty welcome to travelers."

Culling set up a tent for himself and his wife while he and workers dug into the earth.

At 250 feet they struck water and Culling was in business. He sold cool sweet ground water at 25 cents per animal, 50 cents a barrel. After his death in 1878, the business was taken over by his widow's subsequent husband, John Drew.

How the lantern went up depends on the story teller. One story says a near-dead German youth found the station by following a lamplight that Drew was reading by.

Another version holds that Drew decided to set up a permanent beacon after a young man died within shouting distance of the well.

Because Culling's Well was important to Arizona history, the writer launched a search that involved hours and many miles to locate the place. Culling's Well is located north of U.S. 60 between Wenden and Aguila and is on public domain land managed by the federal Bureau of Land Management.

The adventure took on the aspect of hunting for buried treasure, a pot of gold, with the rainbow long since vanished. It would be difficult to give precise directions.

The well was encircled with a three-strand barbed wire fence. Fortunately, the well is at least partially filled. Still, it seemed a long time before a rock tossed inside, hit the bottom.

Culling's Well and its purpose are dead.

A white wing cooed in the distance and other birds called from trees along Centennial Wash. There was nothing more, save the memories of hardy pioneers long ago.

All that remains of Culling's Well—lighthouse on the desert

GOLDROAD
and an old graveyard

The sun, man and inexorable march of time have taken their toll in this ghost town, spawned by man's quest for gold.

Old rock houses without roofs dot the landscape. Mines loom in sundry places and adobe walls melt into the earth. Lizards slither unexpectedly and rock squirrels gambol.

Nonetheless, there's a certain romance to the scene where history occurred. Despite the decay and the man-made scars on the earth, Goldroad has an appeal akin to a deserted village.

History buffs recently had the memory-shaking place to themselves. Only a bird somewhere in the still distance scolded at the intrusion.

Historians note that many buildings were removed or reduced in a dispute between the owners and taxing officials.

There are remains of the huge mill operation overlooking Silver Creek. Mountains of white tailings from the mill operation bespeak of Goldroad's boom days.

It was at the turn of the century that Jose Jerez stumbled onto a gold outgrowth, as the story goes, while he was tracking down stray burros. Jerez was prospecting on a $12.50 grubstake provided by Henry Lovin. One of his claims was named Goldroad. It was sold early in the century and the mine was incorporated.

A post office was established in March, 1906, and was closed in 1942. Four hundred persons were said to have lived here. Two historians observed that mine production had grossed $7.3 million

19

Remnant of long ago cemetery at Goldroad

Goldroad visitor peers into roofless, windowless house.

by the early 1930s.

A story in the *Arizona Republic* in May, 1973, quoted a representative of U V Industries in Salt Lake City stating, "Gold prices in excess of $100 an ounce would justify a closer look at the Goldroad claims, which have been inactive since the outbreak of World War II."

The firm had not increased the pace of exploration it had carried on in Goldroad during the past two years, the story noted.

Our visit to Goldroad had a special target—the cemetery located well away from the town. However, the final resting place was stubbornly elusive, even to a search on foot.

We were about to throw in the sponge, deciding the search in the late May sun better not continue. But one small trail beckoned undeniably.

My husband climbed a mountain knoll to scan the area with binoculars. Suddenly, he straightened up and hollered. "Hold it. Hold it. I think I've spotted it."

Sure enough, there in the distance—like graven images of the past—was a cluster of graves, each enclosed by a picket fence. Close at hand, the little shrines were weathered gray and decayed.

Other graves were outlined simply with stones. Not far from the forlorn memorials was a mine.

Once the goal was attained, we hit the trail back. By the time we traipsed through the sun and desert to reach the car we were parched. Iced tea and orange juice never tasted better.

The ghost town is reached by traveling a lap of old Highway 66 southwest from Kingman, including Sitgreaves Pass. Colorful Oatman is a mere two to three miles away.

HARQUAHALA
nuggets by the hatful

Old adobe buildings slowly weathering away belie the fact that this mining community once boasted a newspaper.

Or that its first saloon grew from a tent with a five-gallon can of whiskey.

And that its mine produced $3,630,000 in gold.

At the ghost town nine miles southwest of Salome, there is an old shanty, its roof so slanting it touches the ground. In fact, the tired old house has collapsed. Other buildings crumble in decay, and a flight of stairs minus the house seems wrapped in old reveries.

Pages of a *Business News* magazine, surprisingly dated 1965, flipped and fluttered in the spring breeze near mine offices. Inside the buidlings, the vandalizing public had made its inroads.

"Ruth and Joe were not here," someone had idiotically inscribed in black paint.

The head frame of a mine and piles of pinkish slag provided mining camp aura.

A forlorn fireplace silhouetted against the azure sky was reminiscent of a once-fine home. Close by, a deep mine shaft gaped near the roadway outside the ghost town. Visitors should be wary of this and other treacherous holes.

Lizards and chipmunks scurried about. In a nearby desert wash, palo verde trees were in brilliant bloom and bees droned in concert.

Gold's discovery here in 1888 spawned a boom town with the usual saloons, boarding houses, a postoffice that opened in 1891, the *Harqua Hala Miner* newspaper and a 20-stamp amalgamation mill.

But before all that—

Nuggets worth up to $300 were picked up off the ground and slabs of gold as big as a man's hand were pried off the rocks when the Harqua Hala mine was discovered in the little Harquahala Mountains.

So wrote Roscoe G. Willson, Arizona pioneer and historian, in 1948.

Three men had staked adjoining claims in the Harquahala area but no especially rich rock was discovered until the day one man ran into a whole nest of nuggets.

He proceeded to gather a hatful, but on checking the location of stakes, Willson's story continued, he discovered the rich find was on the ground of the others. To outmaneuver them, he suggested the three men merge their claims in a three-way partnership. Since the others had not run across the rich streak and knew nothing of it, they

Tired old houses sleep away in Harquahala.

agreed and partnership papers were drawn up in legal form.

Afterward, the conniving one produced the hatful of nuggets. Investigating further, the trio found more nuggets and a "blowout" so rich in gold it was almost beyond belief.

They picked up thousands of dollars in pure gold and found great chunks of float weighing tons, also containing much gold.

"It has been said," Willson wrote, "that no strike in Arizona equaled this value of the surface gold picked up and gathered together with so little effort."

News of the strike was carried in territorial newspapers and in San Francisco and other coast newspapers. As shaft sinking and tunneling progressed, prospectors and mining men flocked in.

Other historians note that around 1898 the ore body was "suffering malnutrition" and the mine was sold at public auction. For the next 35-odd years the Bonanza and Gold Eagle mines at Harquahala were worked by a succession of owners.

As in other mining towns of the Old West, Harquahala's populace moved on, leaving the old buildings behind to shrivel in emptiness and time.

From one old adobe building to another

HUALAPAIS MANSION
worth the rugged hike

An old mansion, its elegance long vanished, clings to a mountainside in a remote recess of the Hualapai Mountains.

Miles from the nearest settlement, the two-story structure was built at great expense to provide comfortable living for owners of the nearby Gold King Mine.

Today, the huge, arched windows gape vacantly. Outside stairways and a balcony that overlooked the mine across the Moss Wash Canyon are mute evidence of once-posh trappings.

A brilliant green vine adds color to the bleak, gray structure. Moss Wash, a live stream, still gurgles below. Inside, the building is empty, the fireplace is dismantled and graffiti mark the walls.

Despite its years of emptiness, the building is fascinating.

Packing in building supplies by mule, probably in the 1930s must have been a tremendous ordeal.

Apparently the Gold King was originally known as the Joseph Stickles mine. A story in the *Mohave Miner* years ago said the Gold King Corp. acquired the seven claims 27 miles from Kingman. The Gold King built a road following the canyon.

In 1929, a 180 foot tunnel had been drifted on a vein of ore and a shaft sunk 50 feet.

The expensive project, the story said, very likely is not a financial success. Still the occupants of the mansion appeared to have a comfortable life with conveniences not usually noted in other mining places.

The building is on property known as the Odle Ranch, which contains 27,000 acres. A good map is essential. The road deteriorates after passing the Odle Ranch headquarters and turning off the "main" road. Our four-wheel drive vehicle growled along the fading trail, marked by high centers, rocks, assorted dips and washes.

Although the mansion was supposed to be two miles away from where the road became impassable, Don and I decided to hike in. The John Lynches, our traveling companions, elected to stay near the car.

The trail worsened, at times disappearing in the creek, then reappearing beyond. The babbling brook, the solitude and the birds calling from the unseen perches combined pleasantly.

Crossing the stream less than two miles from the car, we rounded a bend and there was the mansion.

The house seemed wreathed in the vagaries of mining and remote living. Its windows offer a panoramic view down the stream. There

Hopping a stream on trail to "mansion"

is a vista of the rotting head frame of the old mine.

The occupants enjoyed a fine house tucked into a remote and empty land. They obviously were dependent on the livelihood of the mine.

For a moment we savored the ambience of the house while sharing a can of tomato juice. When we took up the rugged trail, the mansion soon vanished behind.

To make the hike, you should wear comfortable walking shoes and a broad-brimmed hat. Carry a small canteen of water (the creek was running during our jaunt) and a light lunch. The Odle ranch is reached via the Peacock Mountain turnoff from I-40 east of Kingman.

Old "mansion" in Hualapai Mountains

OATMAN
burros and mail call

A Christmas tree with baubles and tinsel glittered in the May afternoon sunlight that filtered through the window at the Oatman Hotel steak house.

The Yule tree is a year 'round perennial in this once-famed mining town on the western slope of the Black Mountains.

"It's Christmas every day in Oatman," explained Trudy Whitaker, the owner. "Let's give gifts of love every day—not just one day out of the year."

One might say Oatman, with its old West background and somewhat ghost town status, is a way of life—unlike any other.

It was Friday afternoon and the town readied for the weekend crowd. Some swapmeeters were already on hand for the Saturday and Sunday tailgate sales and fun.

Elephant's Tooth, a reigning monolith, looks down on the town. Burros could be heard braying down main street, and several of the critters ambled by looking for handouts. A sign on the blacksmith shop said, "Burro food free with a purchase." Burros, a man cautioned, can kick and bite.

"There's about 30 burros that come and go in town," said Larry Crehore, owner of the Skyhawk Antique Shop. "If there is a big crowd, they come in to get fed.

"There's a new beige one that came in the other day. He's still a little afraid of people. Then there's a 'little silver,' about six weeks old, and Dopey, the oldest one in town. He has a crooked jaw. I don't

Nosy burro nuzzles vehicle parked along main street.

A quiet afternoon scene in remote Oatman

think he will be around much longer," Crehore added.

Oatman did not cease existence when the mines closed in the 1940s. In a way, old U.S. Highway 66 from Kingman over the Sitgreaves Pass through Oatman to Topock helped keep the town alive. The opening of the new highway from Kingman to Topock, probably sometime in the 1950s, was a major blow here.

A sign on the side of one store proclaims: "Oatman, Arizona Epitaph. Death of the American Dollar—How the west was lost. Gold mines closed by government order #L208, 1942."

Many shops are closed during the week but open for the weekend. Trudy Whitaker said her steak house is open Friday night, Saturdays and Sundays. The swapmeeters will close down around July Fourth and reopen the Labor Day weekend, she said. A businessman said some shops close during July and August, some remain open the year around.

"We like to think we are the liveliest ghost town in Arizona," Crehore said. "But there is no gasoline available in Oatman. Anyone who comes to Oatman should have enough gas."

Mrs. Whitaker said the old Oatman Hotel no longer functions as a hotel but has been converted into a museum. It is closed because of vandalism and theft, but expected to open soon, she said.

Edward Patchak, whose wife, Yoshiko, is a postmistress here, talked about the new post office he is building.

"It's going to have a porch and benches for convenience of patrons," he said. "The mail arrives here about 11:30 a.m., and by 11 there is a group of Oatmaners around waiting for the mail. The latest gossip is translated at mail time. Everybody knows just about everybody. It is a pretty close knit community. We try to help one another."

Old fire bell frames Elephant's Tooth monolith at Oatman.

SIGNAL
best stores in the Territory

Old trees in fall dress lined the banks of the Big Sandy River as the pickup truck nosed cautiously across the shallow stream.

Nearby dry washes ablaze with yellow-flowered bushes, joshuas, paloverdes and saguaros punctuated rugged terrain set against a background of purple-hued mountains.

The dirt road, veering off U.S. 93, eight miles south of Wikieup, offered new vistas each time it topped a hill. Some 13 miles later, the travelers stopped at a weather-beaten ranch house.

"Where's Signal?" the desert explorer asked, bouncing out of the car to meet the advancing occupant of the house.

"You're in it," the ghost town resident replied.

He was Roy Eaton, and the dog at his heels was Trixie. Inside the yard, Red, a hound, lay unperturbed, while Jeanette, a gentle burro, dozed in the shade of a mesquite.

The travelers had hit their own brand of paydirt. In quest of the ghost town lore, they felt fortunate that Eaton knew the area. Except for a hitch with the military, he had lived here since 1917.

"It was Thanksgiving Day," said Eaton, "and I was 12 when my family came here to live. There was a store, post office, five or six houses, Justice of Peace Gabe Levy, a school. I was one of 22 pupils."

Eaton, working now for the Bill Roer cattle ranch, told the callers where to find remains of two mills operated by the once-flourishing McCracken and Signal silver mines, the cemetery, the old bar. He even warned of an open 90 ft. well in the area.

Roer, who owns the land and has government leases on part of the area, was spotted later corralling range cattle. He was vehement

Old mine and mill near Signal

Old community bar where miners slaked their thirsts

when he spoke of the vandalism inflicted in the area by outsiders:

"I wish that visitors would respect my property and that of other ranchers. If they don't, we will bar the public. That would penalize the good people for the three percent that destroy and vandalize."

Signal was founded in 1877 as a milling town for ore taken from area mines, and some say it once had 800 inhabitants and 200 buildings. It even boasted a brewery during its heyday.

Isolation was a major concern of residents. Goods came by rail from San Francisco to Yuma, then were brought by barge up the Colorado River to Aubrey Landing. The last lap, some 35 miles, was made by mule team. Merchants generally ordered goods six months in advance.

According to a story in the *Arizona Citizen* of Florence on Jan. 11, 1878, as found in the State Capitol Archives, the principal street of Signal was lined on both sides for a distance of several blocks with "commodious and substantial buildings."

"Five general merchandise stores are required to supply the rapidly increasing population," the newspaper stated. "Said stores carry stocks that would be a credit to any town in the Territory."

The paper noted that three large restaurants were in prosperous operation and 13 saloons supplied "the boys" with noted "Noble" and other brands. "Pokaire" was often played.

The Signal Mill was in full blast night and day and there was more than one mine in the area. Another mill was in the offing in nearby New Virginia. Going wage was $2.50 to $4 a day. Butter was scarce even at $1.50 a pound and milk was $1 a gallon.

As with most mining towns, the initial boom and excitement passed, and by the mid-1880s the population had dwindled. Judge Levy, historians note, held the community to a low rate of misdemeanors and felonies because of his record for "extreme" sentences.

Signal's post office was discontinued in 1932, and although some mining activity continued sporadically until much later, mining ghosts apparently have been laid to rest.

Creaking remains of the old Signal Bar, shaded by a gnarled ironwood tree and ruins of two old mills, are mute specters of Signal's past.

A four-wheel-drive or pickup truck is needed to travel a rough, gullied road and cross the river bed to reach one old mill site and the old cemetery. Sometimes the Big Sandy cannot be crossed.

Nearly 50 graves, most of them marked simply by a mound of stones, dot the cemetery. A good-sized cross is etched with colored marbles embedded in concrete to create the name, "A Leivas." The date, "1810-1885."

A lizard slithered across the path of the old mill. The restless wind stirred the sagebrush and mesquite.

Signal basked silent and lonely in its reveries.

Foundations of old mining mill with Big Sandy River in background

Old cross basks in desolation at Signal Cemetery.

SWANSEA
its ore was smelted in Wales

Desert and sagebrush are reclaiming the once-flourishing copper mining town, Swansea, deep in the Buckskin Mountains about 100 miles west and north of Phoenix.

Lizards and chipmunks slither and dart among the decaying shells of buildings in this ghost town, 25 miles from Bouse. More than the usual building remnants dot the main street of the town, started from a mine that, according to historians, produced 27 million pounds of copper from 1908 to 1930.

The road from Bouse (about midway between Hope and Parker) to Swansea (pronounced Swan-cee) winds through hilly terrain, made interesting by cactus, palo verde and purple-cast mountains in the distance. From atop one mountain, Swansea suddenly appears, cradled in a valley, its several buildings basking in the bright sun.

From a distance the houses appear substantial, but closeup looks reveal dilapidated relics. Vandals, who each year destroy more and more Arizona landmarks, have dealt their blow. In the old graveyard, ghouls have removed even the coffins.

Several houses with rock foundations and plastered adobe walls, some with center breezeways, overlook the townsite. A strip of look-alike houses, a stone's throw from the skeleton of the hotel, were probably bachelor quarters for miners.

The decaying old mill, the largest building here, reminds that the admonition on a sign at the entranceway of Swansea is well taken. It said: "Trespass at your own risk."

Originally called Signal, the town was renamed for Swansea, Wales, with the establishment of a post office here in 1909. Ore from northern Yuma and Mohave counties was shipped down the Colorado River and on to smelters in Wales.

The Clara Consolidated Gold and Copper Mining Co., apparently was the original firm. A branch railroad which connected Swansea to Bouse soon provided the camp with a population of several

The ruins of Swansea

hundred. During its prosperous days, the town boasted its own newspaper, *The Swansea Times,* an electric light company, stores, saloons and a justice of the peace.

Historians vary as to when the earlier mine operations shut down. Some say that various mining companies kept the town active until 1924, the year the post office was discontinued. Others state there was mining activity in Swansea as late as the 1940s.

A Bouse resident recalled that the railroad to Swansea was torn up in 1939 and the rail ties sold for 10 cents apiece.

Crumbling mill walls recall better times at Swansea.

SOUTHWESTERN

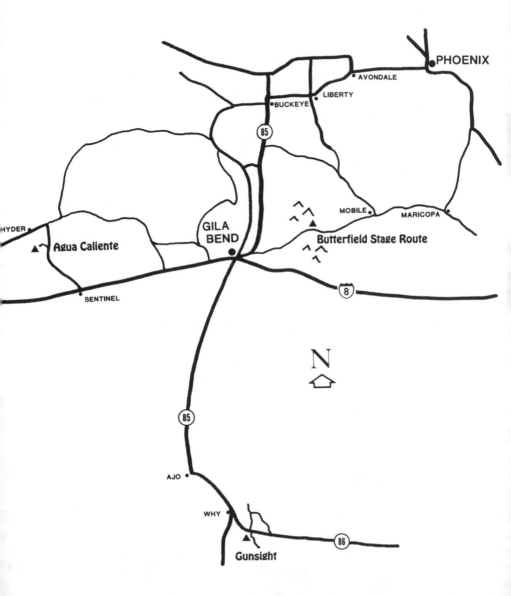

AGUA CALIENTE—
once a pleasant spa

The palm fronds rustled in a breeze off Agua Caliente Mountain in a garden oasis where Mrs. Dolores Conde elegantly preserves a bit of history.

Perched on a little knoll, her home is embellished with wild poinsettias, ferns, cerise-colored bougainvillea and a rock planter she fashioned piece by piece.

But the piece de resistance is her personal museum arranged artistically among century plants and flowers.

Her home is nearby the vintage-old Agua Caliente Hotel, located some 12 miles north of Sentinel, off Interstate 8, west of Gila Bend.

In her relic garden are a pot-bellied stove from the former depot at Sentinel; big black iron kettles that once boiled water for cattle butcherings; skulls of cattle; desert drift wood; rocks and geodes galore.

Mrs. Conde vividly remembers the old resort hotel. There the great, the near-great and commonfolk were attracted mainly because of the hot springs that were known by the Indians centuries ago.

Mrs. Conde worked at the hotel in the late 1930s and early 1940s, but her memories of the hotel go back much farther.

"I can remember as a child seeing Governor Hunt, Arizona's first governor, sitting on the hotel veranda. I remember his big mustache," she said.

The old 22-room hotel, now decaying in gaunt, musty emptiness is a mute reminder of its own heyday. According to Conde, the oldest part of the construction was in 1897, with the kitchen and

Desert artifacts mark garden museum at Conde home.

dining room added in 1907. Conde's father helped build the hotel, he said.

Mrs. Conde worked at the hotel as a waitress and chambermaid, often carrying water by the pitcherful to rooms of hotel guests.

"Guests paid $5 a day for room and board," she said. "My pay was a dollar a day, but I got tips."

Jacobo Sedelmyr is said to have visited the hot springs in 1744. He noted then that the Indians used the warm water springs for medicinal purposes.

The resort hotel was taken over by military officers during World War II, when a training camp was established nearby. The army built the huge swimming pool, which still contains some water.

Still later the old hotel was used by migrant laborers. The hot springs dried up as ranchers irrigated large tracts of land from the wells.

The old hotel, with 18-inch thick plaster-coated adobe walls and high ceilings, contains a few old chairs and tables, a safe, and old kettles. Near the hotel are crumbling bath houses.

An old caretaker added a tale for good measure. "At night," he said, "the floors and doors in the old building squeak, and you can hear the coyotes howl.

"But," he added with conviction, "the hotel isn't haunted."

Plaster and adobe in time-worn patterns and textures—
side view of old Agua Caliente Hotel

BUTTERFIELD STAGE LINE TRAIL — rediscovered

It's a winding trail with washes and jostling dips but it's wreathed in a history that sends the imagination backwards.

The remote little stretch in the Maricopa Mountains is posted as a fragment of the once-famous Butterfield Stage Trail. For hardy souls with the proper vehicles, the route holds a Bicentennial adventure with bracing desert beauty as an extra bonus.

Desert colors are radiant, with mountains wreathed in varying purple haze. Saguaro cacti are profuse in pockets along the trail. Ocotillos seem extra large and palo verde trees are abundant. There is desert mistletoe, greasewood bushes, slithering lizards, chipmunks, rabbits and, of course, snakes.

Arizona Boy Scouts have marked a segment of the Overland Stage Route, helping to recapture the spirit of the trail. Boy Scout camping director Frank Sanders said the 5.75 mile link through the pass in the Maricopa Mountains was established through research as the route used by the Butterfield Stage. He said most of the research was done through the U.S. Forest Service. Boy Scouts started the trail project about six years ago.

"As far as we know it's the real trail," Sanders said.

The Mobile topographic map, dated 1951, depicts the trail as the "probable route of the Butterfield Stage Line." The map is a good adjunct for the trip.

A major portion of the area is protected by the Bureau of Land Management.

In cooler months, Boy Scouts maintain the signs, camp and hike through the pass, but do not camp within a certain distance of the wildlife water storage area.

The desert trail starts some nine miles west of the community of Mobile, off the graded Maricopa-Gila Bend Road (dusty with

West entrance to the trail

39

Boy Scout marker adds historical data.

washes and dips) that parallels the Southern Pacific Railroad line. A "Butterfield Trail" sign marks the east entrance to the trail.

Some four miles north a marker indicates the Butterfield Trail stretch and points west, where the trail traverses a pass in the mountains. After the pass the trail meets another road that goes south to the Maricopa-Gila Bend Road. The distance of the circuit off the Maricopa-Gila Bend Road is about 11 miles.

The trip is rough. It dips through washes and snakes through the Maricopas. On a recent trip, travelers were glad to be in a four-wheel drive vehicle. It is not a trip for passenger cars.

In a few places the trail grows dim or there is more than one trail, all calling for good judgement.

The Overland Stage Route once spanned 2,525 miles from Tipton, Mo., to San Francisco. The 432-mile Arizona section had 18 stops that were from 17 to 45 miles apart. The stages averaged about five miles an hour on the trip, with two stages making the run each way weekly.

Phoenix did not exist in those days. The most northern part of the Arizona lap was at Maricopa Wells and the trail left Arizona to the west of Yuma.

The line was operated by young men. The 1860 census of the Territory of New Mexico, County of Arizona, showed most drivers, mail agents and conductors were in their 30s and 40s. The oldest driver, age 40, was killed by Indians.

Mules and horses were used to pull the carriages. The ratio was four to one in favor of horses. In the operation of the mail, 111 Americans and 57 Mexicans met violent deaths in sending the mail and passengers through. Indians attacked the stages frequently.

The line closed with the outbreak of the Civil War. The route ran through secessionist territory and schedules were canceled.

On a recent trip, travelers were neither passed nor overtaken by another car. The stillness, at times absolute, was interrupted by the cries of birds or an occasional airplane droning in the distance.

GUNSIGHT
silver bonanza

Nestled against a mine-pocked mountain, Gunsight is a fragile remnant of its once-roaring days.

The town, launched by rich mineral lodes and lusty prospectors hoping to get rich quick, drew its name from a nearby mountain with a striking resemblance to a gunsight.

Decaying ruins near the Gunsight mine mark the once-thriving camp, which claimed 1,500 population at its peak. Ruins of the largest house boast a crumbling fireplace and paneless windows offering a panoramic view of the cactus, mesquite and palo verde-studded desert, with a glimpse of mine tailings at Ajo in the distance.

The historic site is roughly 15 miles south of Ajo, near the Papago Indian village of Schunchuli, which means "many chickens." A few scattered houses, an old windmill, mesquite-limb corral and St. Martin Mission Church characterize sleepy Schunchuli.

An old saddle house, a part of the old Gunsight Ranch, is adjacent to the mine area. Inside, a rack bears a lone horse collar. And, in keeping with the name of the village, a few chickens strut casually about.

The largest ruin at the Gunsight camp was the home of the family of C.B. Sheehan, who arrived to work at the Gunsight mine around 1914. Lawrence Sheehan, a Phoenician, was born at Wall's Wells, five miles south of Gunsight.

Sheehan, who lived at Gunsight until 1926, said that the mine produced about $400,000 in silver in its early days. According to historians, the mine was discovered in 1878 by a man named Myers and three others. With some ore yielding as much as $3 a pound, the mine proved "phenomenally rich."

In a report to the director of the mint on statistics on the production of precious metal in 1882, the Gunsight mine was mentioned as one of the best developed and equipped in the territory. The Sheehan mining property was recorded in 1922.

Sheehan said there is evidence among the diggings that the Spaniards beat "modern-day" miners to the site. According to one geologist, "the conspicuous croppings of the veins, some showing galena, nearness to water and trading post at Wall's Wellsand copper croppings of the Ajo region lead to belief that Spaniards and Indians had worked in the area."

The mine was closed, Sheehan said, in 1895, on passage of the Sherman Silver Act.

The mines and Gunsight camp area, including the ruins, are privately owned and closed to the public due to the danger of open mine shafts. One, for instance, is the 700-foot-deep Baker shaft, which yawns openly and is extremely dangerous. Rattlesnakes in mine shafts are another hazard.

Near Schunchuli, the Gunsight Cemetery now is used by the Papagos. There are no headstones, but paper is hung from wires to scare away the evil spirits.

"The king of the Gunsight is buried in that cemetery," Sheehan said. "His real name was George Sayres and he lived in a cave above the mine and went about barefooted. I can remember 'the king' telling tales about shootings in early Gunsight."

Miners and prospectors lived in the houses at the mine and ate in a tent. The elder Sheehan installed a water line to the camp from Wall's Wells, using pumps at intervals to push the water the five-mile stretch.

The mining community first was called Allen or Allen City for the merchants of the camp. The Gunsight Post Office, established in 1892 was discontinued in 1896.

CENTRAL

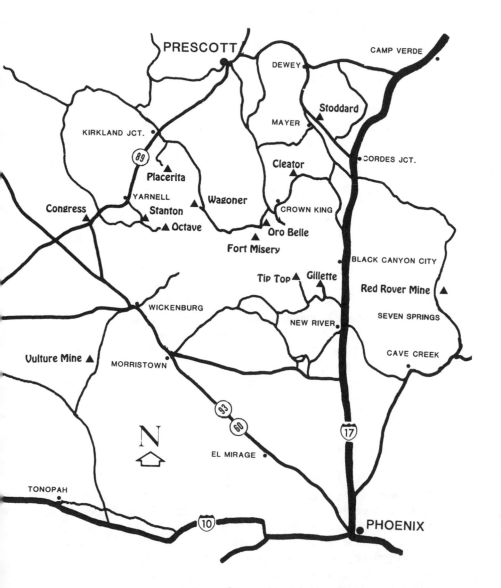

CLEATOR
in the Bradshaws

On a quiet Saturday afternoon, a man sat at Tom Cleator's saloon sipping beer and listening to bar-stool palaver.

"Got any potato chips?" he asked, interrupting the conversation to query Cleator, the bartender.

"What kind do you want? Plain, barbecue or sour cream and onion?" Cleator countered. "We've got everything but smog up here."

A cool breeze from the Bradshaw Mountains sifted in the screened front door that April day.

Cleator owns the 40-acre place that, with a population of 10 and a history a mile long, surely qualifies as a ghost town. The place was owned before him by his father, James Cleator.

Folks keep coming up the dusty road—some 13 bumpy miles that winds off Interstate 17 and spirals up to Crown King. Most visitors migrate to the Cleator Bar. That seems the only place of action.

There are all sorts of memorabilia cluttered about—things like old ice-cream parlor chairs, miners' lamps and bits of bridle tack.

The town has a cluster of old weather-beaten buildings, the bar and a school, the latter built about 1930. Outside the bar, there are 10 mailboxes and a phone booth.

Cleator said most folks in the town of 10 have about that many goats, cats, dogs and probably rattlesnakes. When a guy asked for "two for the road," Cleator dished out a bit of wisdom.

"That usually means two for the ditch," he said.

It was high noon. The clock on the wall still said 10:50, but no one seemed to notice.

A quiet pair ordered two Dr. Peppers and asked the price. Cleator said, "One thin dollar will be enough."

A spectator looked askance when a couple of guys ordered big fat dill pickles to go with their brew. One had a ready explanation.

"Beer-and-pickles is something to do in Cleator," he said, taking a crisp bite for emphasis.

Tom Cleator has lived here a long time.

"I've been here forever plus a day and that's not all my life because I'm not dead yet," said Cleator, busy behind the bar or bounding into another room for more Sprite.

The dill pickle munchers smacked their lips over the pickles. Another patron was so impressed he bought a king-sized pickle— price 30 cents. He even ordered three for the road—pickles, that is.

The conversation veered in another direction as Cleator talked

Bar on Cleator's "main street"

about people who steal things here. Consequently he plans to fence in the town this summer. He also has mining interests in the area, one backed up with a "Notice of Location" dated 1896.

Cleator jokes a lot but he appeared dead serious when he promised dire consequences to anyone caught stealing about his mine.

Back on lighter subjects, Cleator produced a picture of himself and his father standing in front of a 1934 Ford Roadster. The old car's grill hangs on the bar wall.

A Prussian helmet given to his father for selling the most war bonds in Cleator is another memento.

"I never throw anything away," he said. "When you live in one place so long, you don't throw things away. If you do, you might need it sometime."

Cleator had little to say about the beginnings of his town. He said such information could be found in ghost-town books.

The *Arizona Republic* files are informative. James Cleator, born on the Isle of Man in 1870, came to Arizona in 1900 to prospect in the Bradshaws. The railroad was building from Mayer to Crown King in 1902, and by 1905 Cleator bought half interest in a store and saloon at Turkey.

The late historian Roscoe Willson visited here in 1906. Later he wrote that Turkey Siding was established where Cleator now stands. In 1915, Cleator acquired the town from his partner and the post office was changed from Turkey to Cleator.

When Cleator acquired the property, the land was held as unpatented mining claims, six in all. By 1951, and probably long before, the Turkey Creek and Turkey Gobbler mines had been patented.

When James Cleator was 77, he thought of retiring.

A story in *The Republic* reported that the town of Cleator was up for sale and other papers published the story. The owner was flooded with letters of inquiry, but for some reason the sale was not made.

Cleator schoolhouse—a reminder of busier days

CONGRESS
gold in the hills

Visitors shivered in this once-thriving gold-rich mining camp but not from any ghosts. It was the wind, sharp and cold on a November morn.

The only place to find enough protection for a charcoal grill fire at noon was in a deep wash, its sandy bottom marked with quail footprints.

As the charcoal glowed softly and the steaks broiled, the savory aroma filling the air, there was time for reflection on the ghost town's past.

Evidence of mining still looms on the hills, but the old town, some three miles away from today's Congress on U.S. Highway 89, is all but obliterated.

The time was when a 40-stamp mill hugged a foothill of Date Creek Mountains, and the Silver Dollar Saloon echoed with convivial miners.

Umbrella trees lined Main Street and roses bloomed, according to a Prescott newspaper reporter who visited here in 1890. The town had its lively days, but the gold ran out. The inhabitants left. The town died.

Today wood and adobe remnants, the old mine, an ancient cemetery, testify to the camp's souvenir past.

In the past four years, however, there is renewed activity at the Congress Mine. A cyanide leaching plant, its red buildings visible from afar, operates to recover gold in the dump.

Historians and files in the *Arizona Republic* note that the gold lode was discovered by a Dennis May, around 1884. Reportedly, for a period, the mine was sold to a Diamond Jim Reynolds of Mississippi River boat fame. By 1897, there were 425 men employed at the mine. The railroad brought to Congress Junction had a spur to the mine.

Most notable passenger on the spur line was President William McKinley. He was deeply touched when "sturdy" miners greeted him by waving the U.S. flag.

Belle Deck, who lives in the "new" Congress area, was born in Congress. Her keepsake pictures of McKinley on the train also reflect the trees in the mining camp.

Mrs. Deck, daughter of Harry Herskowitz, a grocer in Congress City, lived in an 11-room house that stood on a hill overlooking the town.

Today, the blackened wood from a portion of the 100-year-old house, clutches the hill. Nearby, is still another mine, the Senate or

Three walls—a reminder of the past at old Congress

Mountain View Claim, an extension of the Congress mine. Historians noted the Congress Mine contains deep shafts and honey-combing tunnels.

Congress or Old Congress, as it is sometimes referred to, had upper and lower parts separated by a buffer strip. The upper part contained the mill, company offices, the company store and homes of mine officials. The lower town, some say, was where the "common" people lived.

In 1898, a fire starting in the restaurant next door to the Silver Dollar Saloon, consumed nearly every commercial building in lower Congress. It also claimed two lives.

Stories differ, but about 1910, the ore quality had decreased to a point it was no longer profitable to mine. Ore dumps continued to yield a profit.

Mrs. Deck said Congress had passed its heyday when she was born.

"We lived up on the hill. There wasn't much left downtown. Some buildings were hauled away. I remember the fig trees that were left. When I was a youngster, I climbed the big trees and ate the figs," she said.

In later years, Mrs. Deck said, the mine was leased and there was work in the dumps in the late 1930s. It was then shut down for a long time.

There is a caretaker at the site and much of the area is marked "no trespassing."

The Old Congress Cemetery, probably 100 years old, and containing old tombstones and ornamental fencing around the graves, interests history buffs.

Otherwise, Old Congress is mostly a quiet place where jackrabbits and coyotes roam.

FORT MISERY
a trip back into time

Old Fort Misery basked ever so serenely above dry Humbug Creek. A breeze sighed up the creek stirring tree limbs naked in wintertime desolation.

Ancient trees, their last leaves long since drifted to the dry carpet below, towered majestically over the lone little house.

An old truck cruised along the road that coiled through ghostly Fort Misery, deep in the beautiful Bradshaws.

The tranquil scene laced with memories of Arizona pioneers was one to be savored slowly. It was a time to turn in fancy to yesteryear.

Some observers have surmised that Fort Misery, so marked on topographic maps and forest signs, was once a military fort. Mrs. William Nelson, who was born "up the creek" at the Oro Belle in 1906, however, calls that concept erroneous. She has a different story.

"The house was built by a man named Al Francis," said Mrs. Nelson, now of Glendale. "He came to the country with a team of horses and helped build the railroad at Crown King.

"There never was a fort there. Francis used the 'misery' term as a figure of speech because of the hard times and the loneliness of the remote place.

"Later owners of the property carried on the name," she said.

Mrs. Nelson remembered an old well near the house and fruit trees that flourished at the mountain homesite. She spoke of a tombstone for William Bell, a Civil War veteran, whom the hill folks called "Old Kentuck." He built an unusual home down the creek, partially inside the hill.

49

"It's been years since I've seen the tombstone," Mrs. Nelson said.

Trees guard log cabin at Fort Misery.

"But it's up on a hill in the area."

Her memories, the history, the quaint name, the wild country were ingredients prompting an adventure in the Bradshaws.

Leaving Crown King, the four-wheel drive vehicle trail left the Horse Thief Basin road, skimmed a short way on the old Senator Highway, then veered left on a road marked "Oro Belle, 3 miles, Ft. Misery, 7 miles." The altimeter stood at 6400 feet in the pine-scented forest.

The rugged trail passed by former ghost town Bradshaw City's cemetery (no headstones noted) and descended into the Ore Belle, a "ghost" mining camp. At a later road fork, the left trail headed to Fort Misery, crossing and recrossing Humbug Creek.

Near an old boiler that once generated heat to operate the Gazelle Mine hoist, a deep mine shaft gaped dangerously near the road.

Fort Misery snugged against the hillside beyond scenic Castle Rock, Kentuck's house. Further down the stream was posted "No trespassing."

Search for the old tombstone took time and finally ended at the top of a hill reached by a four-wheel drive trail that stemmed near the house that once belonged to Bell.

The stark, white granite marker among prickly bushes said simply, "Corpl. Wm. Bell, Co. E., 35th Kentucky Mtd. Inf." Mrs. Nelson said that Bell was over age 90 when he died.

"The tombstone arrived by train in Crown King," she recalled. "Al Francis hauled it to Fort Misery in a wagon. He and a man called 'Burro John' set it up on the hill."

Afterwards, the bone-jarring ride to Castle Hot Springs proved no place for greenhorns nor the wrong type vehicles.

GILLETTE
time and the elements take their toll

The old Burfind Hotel lies in rubble and the absolute quiet of this old ghost town is broken by the rustle of the Agua Fria River, a stone's throw away.

And yet, 100 years ago, an 1880 Phoenix newspaper said Gillette "in a not too distant day is designed to be a place of importance with more active mining claims in adjacent mountains."

Gillette is situated on table land some 40 acres on the west bank of the Agua Fria River, which is the boundary at that point between Yavapai and Maricopa Counties. In terms of the old Black Canyon Stage, it was 45 miles out of Phoenix.

Today, in fancy, one can imagine the stage coach driver arriving in a cloud of dust and pulling reins on the horses so passengers could alight at the once fine Burfind Hotel.

Gillette was founded in 1878 by Dan B. Gillette, Jr. (some say Gillett), superintendent of the Tip Top Mine during its heyday. The town was developed because of its 10-stamp mill to process ore from the Tip Top, some nine miles away.

Six streets—Main, California, North, Pine, Mill and Market—and five blocks comprised the town. There were shady streets and modest houses, several stores, saloons. And, as could be expected, there were killings.

A newspaper of that era reported "the town had everything but a jail and a church." Jack Swilling, leader of a party that first settled in the Salt River Valley, lived here.

The late Oscar Wager, an Arizona pioneer, once recalled that his parents operated a stage coach station here. Oscar, at age 13, delivered the mail between Tip Top and Gillette.

James M. Barney, Phoenix historian, quoted a newspaper item that told something about the town:

"I strayed down to Gillette the other day and found the Tip Top mill running all right, the place full of people, and teams and pack trains running in and out. The place is well represented in all kinds of business necessary to supply the wants of the public except in the matter of saloons, there being but four in full blast...."

Gillette, with a post office from 1878 to 1887, started slipping in 1884 when the mill was moved to Tip Top. The town remained as a stopping place on the stage coach line until around 1912. In time, the railroad between Prescott and Phoenix wrought finis to Gillette.

Crumbling ruins of the old Burfind Hotel at Gillette

For a time the old hotel was used as a hub for a dude ranch. Access was difficult and rains filled the Agua Fria River, isolating Gillette.

It isn't easy to reach the place today. It is located roughly about five miles via graded road, then into a Jeep trail, west of the Table Mesa Exchange on Interstate 17. If drivers take the wrong road they can find themselves on dangerously eroded roads. Keeping to the right on the Mica Mule Mine Road will eventually put travelers at the Agua Fria River, the crossing of which can be a hurdle.

The two men in our party studied the river in making a determination to cross it on a sunny April day. The word was "go," and after locking in the four-wheel drive, the vehicle made the crossing easily. A rough four-wheel drive trail to the right then took us into Gillette.

A huge javelina sauntering across the road at one point was a fringe benefit sight. Elsewhere, in the Gillette area were several vehicles, apparently on an overnight camp.

It had been 23 years since the writer visited Gillette. Time and the elements and scavengers had taken their toll.

OCTAVE
mines and an old still

George Dowdy, 88, was content. A sentimental journey from Glendale had returned him to Octave in December, 1966, and the historical Weaver Hills.

He sat in the crisp winter air, a windbreaker snugged about his lean shoulders, felt hat angled low, his feet warmed by a campfire.

Rich Hill loomed majestic and purple-hued, wrapped, like Dowdy, in a reverie of the past. The legions of gold seeking, hard drinking miners who took the rich resources of Rich Hill, long since had vanished. Amid the mesquite and cactus hills were ruins of the mining town of Octave, once filled with fortune seekers.

The embers warmed Dowdy's spirit and whetted his memories of people and episodes of his days as a miner in Octave. Half a century had passed since he first jogged into Octave in a buckboard.

It was in 1916 that Dowdy, born in Comanche County, Texas, received a letter from his father, whom he had not seen in 26 years. His father asked George to join him in Octave and sent $150 for George and his wife and four children to make the journey.

In Phoenix, the Dowdys boarded another train for Congress Junction where they spent the night in the old Williams Hotel. Early the next morning they rode a peddler's wagon the 12-mile, day-long trip to Octave. The peddler stopped along the way to sell beef and wares to the mining camps. The combined fare was $6.

The happy reunion was in a one-room adobe house which still stands in the ghost town. Dowdy's father, as a night watchman at the gold mine, and George, after working in the mine at nearby Stanton, mined in Octave.

A room was added to the house and a cellar helped keep food.

Octave's terrain from paneless, frameless window

Water from Yarnell was piped outside the door and lamps lit the night. Dowdy recalled killing 21 rattlesnakes that summer in his yard.

"Eggs sold at seventy-five cents a dozen," Dowdy said, "and Arbuckles coffee was a luxury at sixty cents a pound. The cottontails were so thick that we carried a salt shaker when we went out. We could kill then with stones, cook and eat them on the spot."

The mining company allowed no saloons in Octave but "sixteen of them once lined this lane," George said with a wave of his hand. "Those miners were heavy drinkers."

The saloons and the attendant women of easy virtue were in an area called Jag-Town The saloons were idle but still standing when the Dowdy family arrived. George said there was "plenty going on" after his arrival. "There was a still in the hills where whiskey was made during prohibition and hauled to Los Angeles," he said.

Historians say the first placer mine was established in Octave in 1863 and later eight men established the mining company, giving the camp its name. The mill was once reputed netting its owners $50,000 a month. After several ownerships it was closed in 1942. Its production had run into millions of dollars.

Dowdy moved his family to Glendale in 1918, but later served two work hitches at Octave, part as day watchman.

ORO BELLE
a trip back in time

Keepsake memories were relived when Marian Nelson paid a visit to this ghost town, deep in the Bradshaw Mountains.

She was born here in 1906 when the Gray Eagle Mine flourished and the wagon road along Humbug Creek was flanked with stores, boarding houses and saloons.

Mrs. Nelson had not revisited her birthplace in 30 years, and anticipated the homecoming with no little excitement.

"There it is! That's the Oro Belle," she exclaimed as the modern car struggled around a mountain curve and crossed a cattle guard. Sure enough, the Oro Belle, basking in the noon sun, nestled serenely in the bottom of a canyon a mile away.

The old store where her father's stage wagon stopped daily with mail and provisions from Crown King, loomed gaunt, its gaping doorway waiting for customers that never come.

The bank vault where gold and silver were stored was still recessed in the mountain, and an old safe rotted in its cool interior. Other

Mrs. Marian Nelson at old Oro Belle store and stage coach stop

Rock wall for Oro Belle road was built by Austrian masons.

souvenir buildings, their open windows looking out at yesteryear vistas, studded the deserted village.

"My first silver dollar came out of that mill," said Mrs. Nelson, the sight of the old mill skeleton awakening memories. "A miner found the dollar and opened a savings account for me in the Yavapai County Savings Bank in Prescott.

"Pancho Villa packed in wood for the woodburning mill," she said, relating handed-down stories from her pioneering family. "At first, everyone thought he was a delightful person, but he couldn't get along with the men. Finally the mine manager, George Harrington, fired him."

There were other recollections. Her uncle, Alfred Champie, daily walked the oil pipe line from the Oro Belle to Crown King, checking for leaks. Another uncle sold a steer to buy Marian a new pair of shoes. And her brother was buried in the cemetery.

Mrs. Nelson left here in her early childhood, but lived in the same general area at Turkey Creek, Horse Thief and Crown King. Periodically she revisited Oro Belle.

"When the mine shut down in 1908, people left by stage coach," she said. "They left dishes, pots and pans, beds, most everything behind. Some buildings were dismantled and hauled away.

"I remember that as a child I returned, roamed through the remaining buildings and imagined that the eyes of former inhabitants were watching me," she said.

Mrs. Nelson remembered that an engineer at the nearby Pacific Mine had a daughter named Rosemary DeCamp (later of movie renown). Big moment for the mining communities came the Fourth of July when the hill people boarded the train at Crown King for the Prescott Rodeo.

"The DeCamps had more money than we did," she said. "Rosemary wore a black taffeta dress with matching taffeta bloomers. I begged for a pair, but my mother told me that taffeta did not smell nice next to the skin."

In the revisit here, the road from Crown King, a five mile distance, required an hour's difficult driving. Built in the 1890s, the road should only be traversed with 4-wheel-drive or truck vehicles.

The trail leaves Crown King, through the pine fragrant forests, then winds into manzanitas, wild laurel, century plants and yerba santa. Along the road were interesting rock wall build-ups constructed, Mrs. Nelson said, by dry-wall masons from Austria.

57

PLACERITA
where Bucky O'Neill once rode

The wind whistling down Main Street flapped loose metal stripping on a decaying building and the sound added an eerie, forlorn atmosphere. Only a few remnants mark Placerita, once a ripsnorting mining camp in the Weaver Mountains east of Peeples Valley.

The four members of our party had been hunting for hours but still the ghost town was elusive. According to our geological survey map, Placerita was in the vicinity, but the mountains and gulch with its gurgling stream did not easily give up the secret.

Finally, one man climbed a hill and, scanning the area with binoculars, discovered remains of a stone foundation. His shout sent the others scrambling—much as though looking for a buried treasure.

The sun was waning over the mountains when we inched through some bushes and found the rock foundation. The real "paydirt" occurred when a rock house was discovered.

The place had a post office for 14 years dating from 1876. The famed Sheriff Bucky O'Neill rode horseback here to arrest a man accused of murder. Placerita Gulch once boasted gold placers.

At the time of our visit the rock house took the spotlight. A concrete marker above the front door read "Isabella—1875." Whoever she was, Isabella must have owned the most substantial house in town. It was the only one still standing. Inside features were a fireplace and a floor with a trap door.

A well gaping hazardously beneath a few old boards and remnants of sundry foundations were other mementos of prior habitation. A

Stone house in Placerita bears name plate "Isabella."

Mill house of rotting wood and sheet metal

stone-headed marker, where two men had staked out and duly recorded claims "for all valuable ore" indicated there may have been something valuable in the hills.

Boarding for home in the early twilight, we were full of speculation about the yesteryear life along the now quiet gulch. Our four-wheel vehicle headed for home, growling its way up and down little washes and hills. Perhaps it was on the same trail that Sheriff O'Neill rode over on his horse that day in the 1880s.

Battered boot found along wagon-width trail—once Placerita's main street.

RED ROVER MINE
shedding light on the past

A cluster of decaying houses is a forlorn remnant of the once lively days of the historic Red Rover mine, 50 miles north of Phoenix.

Loose timbers, dangling cables and assorted sheet iron scraps creak mutely in the wind, and a weatherbeaten house perches aloofly on a cliff.

Long ago the house, set discreetly apart from other crumbling abodes, was occupied by the mine owner. Had he stepped out of the screened porch, he would have dropped down the cliff to the scrub oak and prickly pear studded canyon below.

In one crumbling old house there was a rustle of wings and welcome chirping from a bird, surprised but noisy at the intrusion of people.

Crumbling houses dot main street of Red Rover camp.

Although there was some current activity at the mine in 1969, its origin is clouded in age. Some say the mine was first discovered by Frenchmen in the early 1800s. Others, it was the Spaniards who first ventured there.

Another tale is that the copper-silver mine once produced spectacular riches in silver. One account said that the silver ore from the Red Rover during the last century was so rich it was profitably packed by burros all the way to El Paso.

The road to the Red Rover in many areas still seems geared for burros. Definitely, the trail is for jeeps and pickup trucks. A car would balk at the bumps, dips and creek beds of the trail which coils off a dirt road beyond Seven Springs. Even with a pickup, the five-mile stretch took 50 minutes.

The difficult accessibility probably explains why several buildings still dot hills at the site. The private property is thoroughly posted: "Keep Out—Trespassers will be prosecuted." One reason is the danger in the crumbling old mine shaft.

In the mine's more modern history, there has been a succession of owners and operators. For some years early this century it was owned by Frank A. Gillespie, for whom the Gillespie Dam was named. It is claimed that a complete machine shop is in the lower level of the mine.

E. M. Moore, father of Mrs. Anthony Bennett of Goodyear, began operating in 1927. When the 1929 financial crash struck the nation, the price of copper also fell. The mine closed and did not reopen until 1934. When the family returned to reopen the mine, it was filled with water.

Mrs. Bennett, who lived in one of the houses at the Red Rover for five years, said the mine was "unwatered." When the switch was turned on, an old, still hanging light bulb in the depths of the mine, went on.

"That," Mrs. Bennett said, "was written up in Ripley's Believe It or Not."

STANTON
alongside Rich Hill

Locusts droned in obbligato as dangling old metal, fanned in the breeze from Weaver Mountains, creaked eerily in this old ghost town.

The curious, peering through curtained windows, in a house along "Main Street," were startled by a lizard slithering on the window sill.

And, peering above a half-curtain window in another cottage, it was surprising to see a face returning the stare. The reflection, however, was from an old dresser mirror inside.

Within the padlocked "residential" area, the row of neat houses boasted front and back porches, each opening to mountain vistas. On one, a pink rocking chair rocked in the wind as though propelled by some unseen wraith.

Upon a rise overlooking the townsite was a gleaming white house with windswept verandas and old shade. All were cloaked with restful peacefulness.

Ghost town Stanton, sprawled alongside Rich Hill and steeped in history, may live again. New owners have purchased a 200-acre chunk of the yesteryear town, six miles off highway 89 near Congress.

Nell and Ace Froelich bought the town, with the exception of 10-acres that contain the stagecoach station, hotel and dance hall. This area was awarded to a New Yorker several years ago for writing the winning jingle in a contest sponsored by the *Saturday Evening Post.*

The new owners hope to convert their town into a retirement center and as locale for a new studio for "Ace," an artist.

"Stanton is at its prettiest at dusk," said Mrs. Froelich. "Wickenburg lights may be seen in the distance. And 100 quail sleep in the tall Italian cypress at the corner of our house. Water, allowed to run from our well into Antelope Creek, attracts deer at night."

Stanton, originally called Antelope Station, began with a gold strike on Rich Hill in 1863. The A. H. Peeples party with Pauline Weaver and Jack Swilling, names prominent in Arizona history, was camped and prospecting in the area. A popular historical version records that when a Mexican youth climbed the mountain east of the gulch he found nugget gold barely beneath the earth's surface. It is claimed that men used knives to gouge $100,000 in nugget gold within three months.

That's how Rich Hill, east of Antelope Creek, got its name.

Charles P. Stanton, a ruthless, conniving man, arrived at Antelope

Old Stanton hotel, station and saloon

Station in 1871 and in time became deputy, justice of peace and post-master. He changed the name of the town to Stanton and rode herd on his cutthroat crew, cornering the stage coach trade from Prescott to Wickenburg. His deeds came to an end when he was shot to death for his unwanted attention to a Mexican girl.

Mining engineer George Upton, an uncle of Miss Maurine Sanborn, acquired the gold mining camp nine years after Stanton's death. Years later, Miss Sanborn, a former nurse, arrived to take care of Upton in his later years.

Today all Stanton property is posted against trespassing and a sign in the stage coach station area notes that buildings are condemned.

Lesser known in the area is the reputed Antelope Stage Coach trail that juts off the highway beside a little white church about a mile from Yarnell, near the Ranch House Restaurant. In relatively good condition except for a few "high centers" that require careful driving, the road drops some 2,000 feet in four miles. It winds through Weaver Mountains and terrain marked with catclaw, mesquite, prickly pear and towering century plants.

Jostling over the trail in cars, it was easy to imagine the rugged ride aboard horse-drawn stage coaches. The late William A. Brown, of Sun City, a passenger, had an idea.

"Drive down the trail in second gear," said he, "so that you don't miss anything. Sometimes the deer pose for you along the way."

(Since this story was written, a man reported he was shot at when he went to view Stanton.)

STODDARD
meat hooks remain

Inside the decaying cook house in ghost town Stoddard some modern scribe has written on a wall, "The Acid Wind."

The implication is in doubt, but there can be no doubt that the wind, the sun and time have ravaged Stoddard, erected long ago by miners at the Stoddard-Binghampton and Copper Queen mines.

The ghostly remains are along the Agua Fria River in the Bradshaw Mountains, northeast of Mayer.

The frame loading dock at the stage station, where freight wagons once lumbered to a halt, has collapsed. The crumbling station of rock and concrete is mute testimony of the town's lively days. It is said that twice a week the stage stopped at the loading dock with a welcome cargo of ice cream for the miners.

Up a brushy, cactus-studded hill behind the station is the windowless cook house. The cool interior of the concrete meat house, backed into the mountains, contains a surprise. Giant meat hooks, probably strong enough to hold an entire beef, still hang from the ceiling.

The Stoddard-Binghampton Mine was owned by Isaac Stoddard, who named the mine for his native town in New York. Stoddard was influential in his day, serving as secretary of Arizona Territory from 1901 to 1907.

Records indicate that a post office was established in Stoddard in 1882 and discontinued in 1907. The town can be reached over rough trails by a four-wheel-drive vehicle or pickup truck.

A small trickle of water in the Agua Fria River prompted a Mayer resident to tell a tale about the time the river went on a rampage.

Four Stoddard miners were returning from Prescott, where they had attended a movie. The Agua Fria bed was dry when they left, but during their absence a thunderstorm and rain triggered a flash flood, swamping the river bed.

"I think I hear water," a miner, unaware of the flood, exclaimed on the return trip. It was 11 p.m. and pitch dark. Seconds later, the miners and the car hit the flood-swollen river bed and were lucky to escape with their lives.

The car was swept away and not a piece of it ever was found, the story-teller said.

TIP TOP
more like tumble down

This old ghost town does not live up to its name. It's far from tip top shape.

Roofs on crumbling houses have long since tumbled down. From the looks of deep holes in the cemetery, ghouls may have been here.

The Tip Top Mine discovered in 1875 was so named because it was a tip top prospect.

Oscar Wager, who archives of the Arizona Historical Society say came to the mining camp in 1884, said that the mining camp had about 200 people. Many were servicemen of the Civil war—both North and South.

Wager said they got along very well. Most had mining claims. Freight trains with 16 to 17 mules made weekly trips to Phoenix hauling supplies in, ore out. And there was a grade school for 15.

The camp in those early days consisted of two general stores, six saloons, two restaurants, a Chinese laundry, a feed yard and assay office.

A post office was established first in 1879 and the last discontinued in 1895. Wager, as a teenager, carried mail between Tip Top and Gillette three times per week—by horse, burro and buckboard.

Wager reported that two men were killed in gunfights, one by lightning and one by a centipede.

It seems that the miner, pulling on his boot, was "bitten on the toe." He was rushed to the nearest saloon and drank a quart of whiskey. People in those days were not sure whether the centipede or the whiskey killed him.

Probably few people would want to make the trip here. After veering from a dusty road off the Black Canyon Highway at Table Top Mesa exit it is not long before the Agua Fria River crossing. On a recent trip, the river was dry and the crossing made without fear of water or quicksand.

After a turn off on a narrow trail, the next several miles were four-wheel drive country. There were areas where the vehicle crawled through water in a stream bed, crossed dry washes, inched along to avoid high centers and sundry holes and sharp dropoffs from the sides of the road in the high country.

Mesquite, cactus and paloverde trees basked in beauty in the fall sun. Stopping for a coffee break, the only noise in the early morning was a chattering covey of quail.

Other visitors prowled about the buildings, remembering rattle-snakes of a previous visit. Several old mines are reportedly in the

Miner's shack crumbling away at Tip Top

area, one not far above "main street." And across the trail from an old house was a deep concrete-lined excavation.

Eating lunch in the shade of a mesquite tree, visitor thoughts turned again to the old days.

Wager said that during his time here, there were occasional dances but the camp was short on women.

"Once a minister came from Phoenix to save sinners," Wager remembered. "The services were held under a cottonwood tree and the miners brought their beer and enjoyed the service."

It seems, though, that the men contributed generously when the collection plate was passed.

VULTURE MINE
Henry Wickenburg's haunts

It was March and time was drawing near for the annual return of the vultures from their winter sojourn in Mexico.

So predicted Jim Osborne, one of the managers of the historic Vulture Mine and camp, which were started after Henry Wickenburg discovered gold here in 1863.

Osborne expected the vultures to arrive about April 1. He described how they prepare for their return to Mexico at the onset of cold weather.

"For several days when the vultures are ready to go south they start spiraling, maybe two dozen of them," he said. "They go higher and higher, but come back down if air currents aren't just right. Finally, they take off."

One of several versions of the story of how Wickenburg found the gold is that he shot a vulture and it fell by a nugget.

The Vulture Mine, which produced millions of dollars in gold ore, now basks in silence. The mining camp includes an ancient school house, assay office, glory hole, assorted mine buildings and even a hanging tree.

The mine is about 12 miles from a turnoff 2.5 miles west of Wickenburg on State Route 60. The graded road to the camp winds through hills and washes with expanses of saguaro and other cacti.

According to records of the U.S. Department of the Interior, the mine is part of an area that was surveyed and patented in 1882 as Vulture City.

At Vulture Roost, the entrance to the tourist attraction, visitors pay the entrance fee and obtain a copy of *The Vulture Trail* for a self-guided tour.

67

Along the trail are a gold-panning area, the blacksmith shop and the gaping glory hole. Visitors are asked to stay on the trail and be careful. There are other holes in the area.

"Seven men and 12 burros are buried somewhere in the depths through a 1923 tragedy," reads one sign.

"The shaft was worked to 2,100 feet but extends to 3,000 foot level through side tunnels," another says.

There are the old cyanide storage building, the process plant where material was pumped from leaching tanks below, the ball mill and the power house with a big diesel engine shipped here in parts and assembled in 1904.

Then there's a one-room adobe-and-rock house with rifle portholes in the walls. Wickenburg is said to have lived there for a time before it became a jail.

The spreading ironwood tree fronting the house is labeled "the hanging tree" where 13 men met their fate.

In the mess hall building, there is a refrigerator against the wall. Pots, pans and dust top the kitchen stove. A sign notes that 50 to 100 miners dined there. Mail call was on the doorstep.

A large picnic area with tables and rusty grills is by the old school house.

Panning for gold means an extra fee. Hours and days the place is open varies according to the season.

WAGONER
wild town no more

The Hassayampa River and rustic, sprawling ranches combine pastorally in the approach to this community from Walnut Grove.

And, as an historic dish, flavored with its own Old West tales, Wagoner is no slouch. There is much left, however, of its yesteryears as a community center.

The old store with its hand-pump gasoline tank has bowed to age and elements. Across the road there is a rotting old bus that once served as a home, a windmill and water tank. And down the road a few paces is a wood building that was the post office.

Gone are the two-story hotel with 10 rooms, the barn with stalls for stagecoach horses and the dance hall. Gone, too, are the miners who once depended on the store for supplies and liquor.

But four old buckboard wheels, also rotting, remain. And therein lies a tale.

Mrs. Nel Cooper, who has lived in the Wagoner area for 48 years, has written about area history.

"That buckboard," said she, "came all the way from Guthrie in Territorial Oklahoma to Prescott in Territorial Arizona."

The story is that the buckboard was piloted by a Horace Cole with a son of President McKinley as passenger. It took the four-wheeler six weeks to make the trek. The carriage met with so many obstacles that McKinley left and boarded a train. But, Cole reached his destination first.

But before that, the town was named for Jaye Edward Wagoner, who founded the community in the early 1800s and evidently was the first proprietor of the store. His wife Minerva was postmaster. 69

Wagoner also ran the saloon and hotel successfully. Construction of Walnut Grove Dam, about a mile south of the town, was a factor.

"Wagoner was a busy place," Mrs. Cooper said. "It was often referred to as 'wild Wagoner.' There were fights and killings in the area. Wagoner itself claims only three killings."

Wagoner sold out and moved to California. The dam, after 10 years construction, was finished about 1888 only to be washed out two years later by a flood.

"By the early 90's," Mrs. Cooper said, "the heyday of gold miners in the area was about to pass." Eventually, Wagoner fell into the hands of McKinley, who came to the area and worked gold claims. Horace Cole was his employe.

"The story goes," said Mrs. Cooper, "that when McKinley found gold too scarce and the store no longer a stage-change stop, he left Wagoner to Cole to pay his back salary."

Mrs. Cooper said the hotel burned in October 1942, the dance hall was brought to an end by fire in 1948, and the barn finally fell to the elements. The store building is now owned by a Phoenician.

Dates on the earliest homesteads patented in the Wagoner-Walnut Grove country indicate the area was settled in 1864.

Today, the many ranches in the Walnut Grove-Wagoner area are very much alive. Wagoner is reached by a marked turnoff just before Kirkland Junction on the White Spar Road to Prescott (U.S. 89). The graveled road winds along the river for a time. At one point, there is a bridge over the Hassayampa, and at another, old shade arches over the road.

On a May day in 1971, folks were congregated about the mailbox talking about a rabid coyote that had attacked an area rancher.

The annual advent of the Desert Caballeros for campout and riding each April causes excitement here. But, mostly, Wagoner is quiet and peaceful, basking in a climate the hill people are apt to brag about.

EASTERN

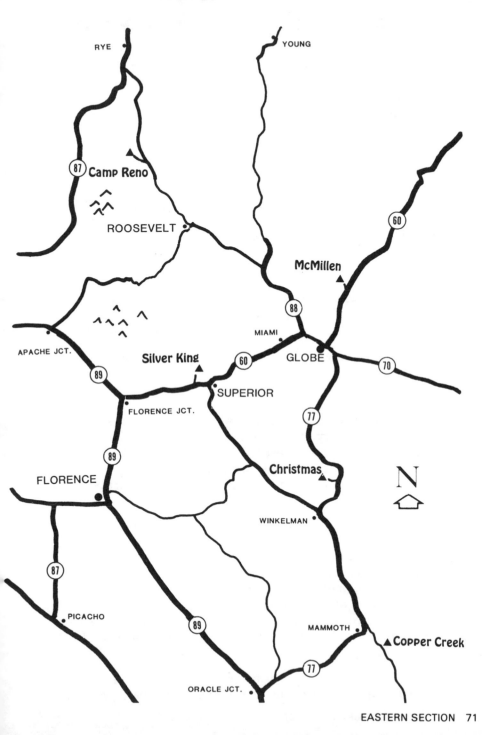

CAMP RENO
scene of Big Dry Wash battle

It was 4:30 on a bright April afternoon when our Jeep rolled into Punkin Center, its occupants dusty from travel along the Roosevelt Lake Road.

Already patrons were stooled up to the bar in the country store where we inquired the way to Camp Reno.

A store attendant asked first—what kind of car we were driving. Learning we were in a four-wheel drive vehicle, she helpfully related directions.

Actually the trip was launched because of a brochure, "Discover Gila County," published by the Globe Chamber of Commerce. It describes Old Camp Reno as one of the historical attractions of the county and a place to explore.

In Globe, the Chamber advised contact at the Punkin Center Store for specific directions to the old camp.

Meantime, we took the Roosevelt Lake route to Punkin Center. The lake, brimming with water from winter snow runoffs, was more blue than the sky. Yellow daisies along the road added other color.

At Punkin Center, we learned Camp Reno was about 3½ miles to the west.

"Old adobe walls are gone. People just picked and picked away," we were told.

The small trail was rough, narrow, full of chuck holes, rocks. It is 4-wheel drive country. High-powered vehicles capable of maneuvering over high center areas are needed.

The terrain in the Mazatzal Mountains is fabulous—cedars, mesquite, roadrunners, running creek, staring cattle, dense trees, tall shade, thickets.

Around one curve, a brushwood barricade brought the end of the road. Camp Reno, however, was at hand, and so proclaimed by a Tonto National Forest sign.

A soft breeze stirred the tall wild grass, cattle bawled in the background. Giant gnarled trees were arched and bent. A large concrete platform spoke of busier days.

It was hard to imagine the tranquil scene today as the place where in 1868 soldiers marshalled for battle against the Apaches in the battle of Big Dry Wash.

Some say Camp Reno was named for Brig. Gen. Marcus Albert Reno. By Sept. 1868, five companies were stationed here. Their mission

was to hold the Apaches in check.

The late historian Roscoe Willson, who wrote for the *Arizona Republic's Days and Ways,* said the camp was named for Jesse I. Reno, who was killed in Turner's Gap in 1862. The camp was an adjunct of Fort McDowell so that troops could be stationed closer to the scene of trouble.

Arizona Place Names notes the post was in a bad location, fully exposed to an open mesa. On either side were deep canyons with water and brush that afforded concealment for Indians. The post died in 1870 as the scene of major Indian confrontations moved elsewhere.

The place was all but deserted for a time, but 10 years later a post office named Reno was established, indicating a small settlement.

Today, the forest scene is quiet and serene. Its secrets are in the past.

CHRISTMAS
postmark of the past

Yes, Virginia, there is a Christmas.

It hugs Dripping Spring Mountains, where quail frolic among the cactus and sagebrush five miles from Winkelman.

The community that sprouted and died so many times, according to the ups and downs of the copper mines, is a mere shadow of its livelier days.

As a town, Christmas is a ghost.

The click of the gambling wheel in the Silver Dollar gambling hall is gone. So, too, is the revelry in the Crystal Palace Saloon, and the music from the Gilded Cage Opera House is stilled.

Those buildings are but memories. The sagging store building, two crumbling houses and the old Christmas mine mill are remnants of the old days.

The empty store, which housed the former post office, is festooned with fading advertisements. In its day, the post office knew a measure of fame. It was flooded in the Yuletide with letters from throughout the nation to be postmarked "Christmas."

As a mining camp, Christmas is very much alive.

Fifteen families live here. Dogs bark at the intrusion of strangers, and there is the constant drone of ore trucks plying from the open pit mine in the distance. At noon the mine horn blasts off, signaling the lunch hour for the 300 workers.

Douglas Middleton, general superintendent of the Inspiration Consolidated Copper Co.'s Christmas Division, said that the open pit copper mine operates 24 hours a day, seven days a week. The underground mine, which brought new life to the camp in the late fifties, closed in 1966.

"People still come here with letters to mail," Mrs. D. H. Wright, a 15-year resident here, said, "but the post office closed years ago."

At the home of the Bart Alvarados, Christmas dinner had been in the making for weeks—ever since their children received a baby turkey last Easter.

"That turkey has grown so big," said Mrs. Alvarado eyeing the bird in the backyard pen, "that it won't go in my oven. I'm going to barbecue him.

A share of Christmas decorations for her little brown house will come from the trees along the banks of the Gila River near Dudleyville.

"We'll make a trip to gather mistletoe," she said. "It makes beautiful fresh wreaths."

The Bud Maniers, who with their son, Scott, 4, live in one of the several modern houses constructed here in 1964, said there was much socializing in the camp.

"We make our own entertainment here," said Mrs. Manier, "since we are removed from towns. There will be lots of Christmas parties."

It may be said that Christmas began on Christmas Day.

The original (about 1880) claims of the mine were acquired by a mining firm representative and several small furnaces located at the site. Mining was stopped when the claims were found to be on the San Carlos Indian Reservation.

The firm petitioned Congress for a boundary change, a move in which another firm was involved, according to a report in the *Arizona Republic.*

The story with all the overtures of the colorful Wild West becomes involved. But in the finale, George Chittenden received a tipoff telegram of the change approval on Christmas Eve. He and his partner arrived Christmas Day and staked claims.

Of course, they called the place Christmas.

(The *Arizona Republic* reported that the mine, closed in 1977 during a strike amid plummeting prices, reopened in April, 1979).

75

Overlooking Christmas mine mill from veranda of old school

RETURN
RIGHT HAND

Old store housed popular Christmas post office.

Old and new mine buildings at Christmas

COPPER CREEK
and SIBLEY CASTLE

Sycamore leaves rustle in the breeze in the rugged, colorful Galiuro Mountains. A brook gurgles. There are mines and ore chutes to view but avoid, and abandoned narrow-gauge rail tracks. Quail and other birds chatter. The trail is barely visible at times or is narrow, one-car size.

All this and much more were meshed during a fall trek to the old Copper Creek Mine camp site and the Sibley Castle.

And, it spelled adventure.

A Valley foursome spent the night in Mammoth, about 100 miles southeast of Phoenix, to get a head start on travel to the camp. The night in the cordial little town was pleasant. Accommodations were at the Sierra Vista Motel, and we had a steak dinner at the Redwood Inn and breakfast coffee in our room.

At a market and gasoline stop, a friendly clerk said, "Watch out for deer hunters. The hills are full of them."

The gravel road to Copper Creek camp proved to be no major problem despite its dips, washes and dust. The scenery—the old mill and mining camp site with creek not far away—was enough to satisfy the travel appetite.

Only fragments remained of the old mining camp launched in 1863. Its first ore—from the Yellow bird claim—was silver, but underlying veins turned sharply to copper.

A water tank topped a hill and a decaying foundation of the post office read "Copper Creek." Unbelievably, the post office established in 1906 survived until Aug. 31, 1942.

But the Sibley Castle quest lay ahead. We might never have reached it were it not for the unexpected arrival of a Tucson four-wheel drive convoy gunning for the same spot.

"Lock in and deflate," their wagonmaster advised before the queue set out for a rugged trail, including the creek bed. Earlier, the leader told our party about a longer route that our four-wheeler could negotiate, except for a short hike.

One hairpin turn near the top of a mountain required three backups, and thoughts of an oncoming car produced shudders. Finally, after rounding a crest, we spied the castle below. It was time to bail out and walk.

On close inspection, the two-story structure, built around 1908, proved to be a rock-and-masonry shell with cracked areas. Still, there was evidence of its former elegance. Arizona Historical Society files note that the home once contained 20 rooms and polished oak floors.

E. Roy Sibley was manager of the Copper Creek Mine, and his wife, Belle, was postmaster. The home was no doubt a social hub.

The Sibleys left around 1910, and the company was reorganized as the Copper State Mining Co. As early as 1922, the mansion was vacated, its flooring transplanted elsewhere. A building across the creek could have been a storeroom.

The skeleton buildings made us wonder what the site was like in other days. The quiet scene is fascinating.

But thoughts of the difficult return kept surfacing. A family in a camper, failing to negotiate the steep hill out, was repairing a tire for a new attack. The convoy trekkers had not arrived. (It was later learned they did eventually reach the site).

Alas, on the return trip, our vehicle gas tank was ruptured. Fortunately, the vehicle carries two tanks.

Dismay over the tank was all but eclipsed with safe arrival back in Copper Creek ghost camp. Music from the creek soothed ragged nerves.

It was a good time to open picnic baskets and remember the Sibley Castle from a safe distance.

Children visit the Sibley Castle in the Galiuro Mountains.

McMILLEN
no matter how you spell it—
it's silver

There's nothing left of things that used to be in this ghost town except a souvenir-old mine, crumbling rock wall and historical marker beside the highway.

While there's no future to McMillen—sometimes called McMillenville, McMillan, McMillanville—it does have a past. And, all because old Charlie McMillen—dead tired (some historians indicate he was a little in his cups) stopped here for a snooze. Settling in

mesquite tree shade, prospector McMillen was soon lost in sleep that March day in 1876.

McMillen and his young partner, Theodore Harris, had left Globe mounted and with three pack mules, enroute to prospect in the White Mountains.

Harris was disgruntled, anxious to be on with the mission when his partner took time out. In his impatience, Harris traipsed about the terrain aimlessly picking into the moss-covered ledge.

A dislodged rock, unseemingly heavy, caught his attention. He awakened McMillen, holding the rock for his inspection. McMillen, the story goes, was immediately alert. The prospector knew his metals and, after detailed scrutiny, his verdict was "silver ore."

Word got about and there was an exodus from Globe. The discovery was called the "Stonewall Jackson." The blossoming camp was named McMillen and in 1877 there were 300 inhabitants.

McMillen and Harris, however, sold out to a California company. The owners of the Stonewall later exhibited in San Francisco specimens with silver ore valued at $65,550—about $1900 per ton, some reports say. In all, about $3 million in silver was produced here.

In time there were a 10-stamp mill and more residents. McMillen was labeled the largest, most substantially built mining camp in the territory. There were several saloons (naturally), adobe store buildings, a hotel.

Other mines were producing in the area. Surrounding camps were called Richmond Basin, Pioneer and Rambro.

An historical marker in tribute to the long dead town stands today besides U.S. 60, about 13 miles north and east of Globe from the intersection of U.S. 60 and 70.

A little trail not far from the highway marker leads to the old mine, perched on the hillside, its entrance half closed. Elsewhere, the quiet is interrupted by a gurgling stream obviously heavily patronized by cattle.

It's hard to imagine there were riproaring times—like the Christmas tree decked out with "cigars, tobacco, grub and bottles of whiskey." A release several years ago from the Arizona Highway Department told of visits from the Billy the Kid Gang to McMillen.

The camp hit its peak in 1880, and the bonanza pay streak played out in 1885. The mines shut down. A few musty buildings survived for a time but have long since vanished.

SILVER KING
faded ruins trigger memories in old silver camp

It was a cold January day when visitors stepped from the car to walk shiveringly into this old ghost town.

The steady climb was complicated by a strong headwind, assorted cameras, jackets and headgear. Hikers were goaded by thoughts of the discovery here and the town's exciting past.

Around a bend in the trail a two-story house loomed forlornly. In a closeup look, an old door creaked and slammed in the wind, casting an eerie aura over the decaying building.

A short distance away is an open mine shaft and another mine shaft was noted in the area.

The road into the area was barricaded and a sign said, "No trespassing—Blasting."

Mike Guzman, Sr., owns the property near Superior, and his permission is required for access.

Crumbling ruins of other structures are scattered about.

Silver was discovered here in 1875—a lot of silver. The strike soon attracted the attention of fortune hunters from around the world. But by 1888 the boom was over.

Perry Wildman, a town merchant in Silver King's heyday, recorded the town atmosphere in writings preserved by the Arizona Historical Society in Tucson.

The residents were mostly Cornish, Wildman wrote, with a sprinkling of nearly every other nationality. The town was isolated without telegraph service to the outside world or to the nearest railroad, which was 55 miles away.

A post office was established in 1877. Wildman said saloon keeper Ed Thompson acted as postmaster.

"When the mail arrived the sack was emptied on one end of the bar and we would pick out our own mail," Wildman said.

Later Wildman became postmaster and installed private boxes in his store.

"Silver King was quiet and orderly," he said. "No acts of violence —except one murder—occurred during my seven years in camp. We were a peaceful, contented, happy people.

"Each man was a law unto himself and anything unruly was not tolerated. We never locked our doors and robbery was unknown.

Gambling was wide open, but always on the square."

Water was a scarce commodity, Wildman said. It was brought in by pack animals and delivered to homes at five cents a gallon for cooking and drinking.

When residents wanted a bath—or others told them it was time— they went to the mine and caught condensed water from the boilers. Or they waited until it rained and caught water as it ran off the roof of the house.

In 1883, however, there was a cloudburst that nearly put a premature end to the community. Residents made for higher ground to save themselves, but one miner was caught in his cabin and washed away. His body was later recovered about 19 miles away.

"We had no resident minister or padre in camp and as it was necessary to have the burial as soon as possible, I was chosen to officiate at the miner's funeral."

Wildman said the mine reached its production zenith in 1886. "All around the vicinity, prospecting and mining was at its height," he said.

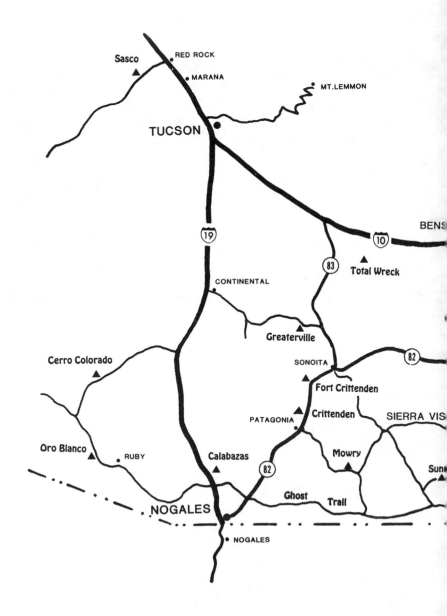

Sasco
RED ROCK
MARANA
MT.LEMMON
TUCSON
BENS
19
10
83 Total Wreck
CONTINENTAL
Greaterville
Cerro Colorado
SONOITA
82
Fort Crittenden
Crittenden
PATAGONIA
SIERRA VIS
Oro Blanco
RUBY
Calabazas
Mowry
Sun
82
NOGALES
Ghost Trail
NOGALES

SOUTHERN

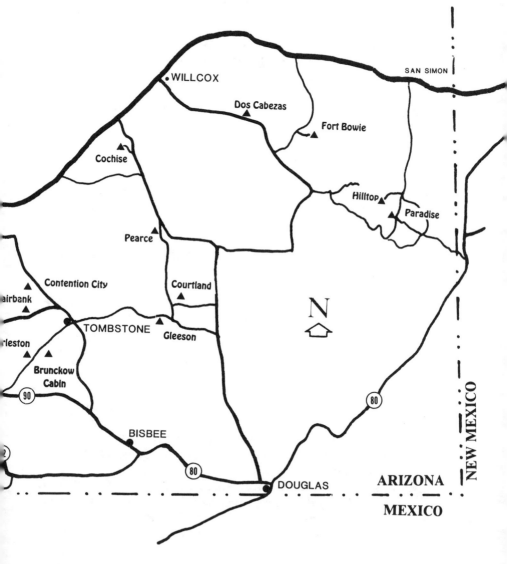

THE BRUNCKOW CABIN
bloodiest in Arizona

Oddly, one of the ghostliest spots in Arizona is not a ghost town. Rather, it lurks around a roofless adobe house perched on a knoll, some 200 yards south of the Charleston highway and a half-mile east of the San Pedro River. Imagine, a place that miners—more than 100 years ago—avoided like a plague.

Labeled the Brunckow house, it is hailed by some as "the bloodiest cabin in Arizona's history."

An Arizona Historical Society file reveals that an *Arizona Democrat* reporter on May 20, 1891, wrote:

"Many will tell you that the unquiet spirits of the departed ones are wont to revisit the glimpses of the moon and wander about the scene which witnesses their untimely taking off. The graves lie thick around the place."

Naturally, such a stage is challenging.

The writer and three others on a cold January day set forth from Tombstone for the Brunckow cabin.

The wind howled fiercely—it so often does on ghost town quests—as we approached the historic house—what's left of it. The structure can easily be seen from the Charleston Road between Tombstone and Sierra Vista.

The Jeep had bounced over a little trail through an area pocked with glory holes and old mines to reach the cabin. The wild, dry grass bowed low in the wind and black leafless limbs of mesquite trees quivered. Sometimes the wind shrieked like a mournful banshee.

It was time to think more about the cabin's background.

The builder was Fredrick Brunckow, a German mining engineer, who was murdered in 1860 and his body found in a mine shaft in the area.

According to one source, William Williams, one of the three Anglos among the several Mexicans at the Brunckow camp, went to Fort Buchanan for supplies in Sept., 1860. He returned after dark to a gruesome find—two Anglos murdered in the cabin. Brunckow was found dead later in the mine. Some say the three were murdered by employes.

Many years later, the *Tombstone Prospector* on May 20, 1897, said that in the early days the Brunckow mine was the scene of much excitement, shootings, and dissension among the owners.

"One man was supposed to have been shot and thrown into a well but as there were abundant men in those days an investigation seemed needless," the writer said.

Brunckow, well-educated, emigrated to the U.S. in 1850. He

The adobe walls of Brunckow cabin losing their battle to Arizona weather.

joined the Sonora Exploring and Mining Co. and worked in explorations in the Tubac area. He developed his San Pedro Silver Mine a short distance from the river. It is probable he built the house on the mound for the greater visibility afforded.

The Arizona Democrat reported the Brunckow property was a place of violence and murder. After Brunckow's demise, there were "no less than 17 murdered on the property."

Even today the house seems wreathed in gloom. Inside, the fireplace was the only adornment that survived time.

It was at the fireplace, according to a lifetime Tombstone resident, that Ed Schieffelin melted and assayed the ore from the mines that were later to bring Tombstone into existence.

Browsing about the adobe, the cabin's storybook dark past emerged. At lunchtime, the weather forced us inside the Jeep to munch on canned Vienna sausages and cheese and welcome drafts of hot coffee.

The wind shook the vehicle atop the little hill.

It could be that not all the shivers of the occupants were due to the cold or the wind.

Ed Schieffelin is said to have assayed ore in this fireplace before Tombstone was born.

CALABAZAS
too old to touch

Unlike most ghostly village remnants, this historic spot was not born through man's quest for precious metals.

Historically, it dates back to the late 1600s. Its role changed kaleidoscopically—mission visita, rancherita, use by the military. All this plus an area boom town that hoped for port of entry status. That designation went to Nogales instead, and gradual abandonment followed.

Today, the sun-baked ruins of the old mission chapel are fenced in on a wind-swept rise, the silent melting adobe reflecting none of its lively past.

But, there is new interest here. Recently, the Arizona Historical Society announced:

"The adobe ruins of Calabazas given to the AHS in 1974, are now in the process of being repaired and stabilized under a state appropriation of $15,000 to arrest deterioration of the one-time mission visita."

Calabazas, sometimes spelled Calabasas, became part of the U.S. through the Gadsden Purchase.

An Aug. 4, 1855 news story in the *San Francisco Weekly Chronicle* and datelined "Calabasas in the Gadsden Purchase," is in files at the Arizona Historical Society.

It speaks of the chief building at Calabazas as the citadel with walls about 20 feet high, unbroken except by a solitary doorway, with heavy doors. A nearby bell gave the alarm when hostile Indians approached.

"If the valley were protected by the presence of a detachment of American soldiers, the land near Calabazas would soon be tilled. Besides there are rich copper and silver mines in the vicinity, which ought to be wrought. . . ." the paper said.

There is confusion in the spelling of the name.

Don Bufkin, assistant to the director of the Arizona Historical Society, said there are two different places within the historical site. He said the town, that once boasted a two story hotel, probably was a mile from the mission site. Nothing is left of the town.

The use of "z" in the name had a longer period of use reference in Spanish documents. Neither spelling is in error, neither is totally right, Bufkin said.

The name Calabazas, (Spanish for pumpkins) applies to the broad area and to try to be too definitive where each name applies would be misinforming, Bufkin said.

The *Arizona Daily Star,* reporting a visit here by the Arizona

Remains of ancient visita chapel at Calabazas

Pioneers Historical Society officers in April, 1940, said Calabazas was not to be confused with the boom town, Calabasas, which flourished in American times.

"The original Calabazas," the article said, "was a small Spanish settlement said to have been visited by the Jesuits in 1763. Gandara, one-time Governor of Sonora, owned it in 1850. It lies nearly two miles south toward Nogales from the boom town.

"The boom town thought it would be the entry port into Mexico and, when the Southern Pacific Railroad line was proposed to go through it, much development began.... The town died about 1883 while Nogales flourished as the border town," the story continued.

The late Roscoe Willson, Arizona historian wrote:

"Calabasas, a rancherita, became an important way point for incoming soldiers, settlers and missionaries on their way north to the Presidio in Tubac. Prior to the Civil War, troops were stationed there a short time."

Recently, an archeologist working at the site said relics found here indicate Indians may have lived at the scene before the mission was built in the 1700s.

Calabazas is some 10 miles north of Nogales, and reached by the Calabazas exit off I 19, then local inquiry about exact directions. **Visitors are discouraged.**

The ruins are closed to the public, completely enclosed with tall cyclone fence topped with barbed wire. Dense mesquite trees, cooperating in guarding the place, crowd around to all but eclipse the ancient structure. Gnats buzz around eyes and ears of spectators who would tarry a while.

Although Calabazas is removed from ghost town fans, it can be savored as an interesting chapter in "things old" in Arizona.

CERRO COLORADO
memories of a silver boom

Crumbling adobe walls bearing the aura of age along with assorted mine shafts today are mute reminders of this ghost town's once-bustling past.

Ghost town sites with satisfying physical remains are getting rarer and rarer. But, the Heintzelman mine here was so important in early area history that just being on the scene is reward to a history buff.

A news account written in 1865 in the Hartford, Conn., *Evening Press* (as noted at Arizona Historical Society files) set the atmosphere, and, in imagination, it was easy to hearken back.

"It was sundown and the plaza of the Cerro Colorado hacienda bustled with activity. The last of a string of huge Sonora wagons were unloading. Herds were driven by the Papago Indians, little Mexican carts were discharging corn into the granary," the story said.

"Team animals were fed by nosebags, making the air hideous with the noise as their food came down. The noise of the hammers and iron in the blacksmith shop, the creaking of the mule power hoisting ore out of a perpendicular shaft of the Heintzelman mine vein. . . ."

Historical accounts do vary. In J. Ross Brown's book, *Tour Through Arizona in 1864*, he noted the village was "silent, desolate, a picture of utter abandonment.

"The adobe houses were fast falling in ruin, the engines no longer at work, the rich piles of ore lying in front of shafts had been sacked and robbed by marauding Mexicans. It is the opinion of S. F. Butterworth and others that the lode is one of the richest in Arizona and will under a judicious system of working amply repay the capital invested in its development."

Apparently, the dormant state of Cerro Colorado then is explained by Brown: "During the summer of 1861 when the federal troops were withdrawn (during the Civil War), the Apaches renewed their depradations and the barbarous races of Sonora turned loose to complete the work of destruction. Mr. Poston's brother, who was in charge of the Heintzelman mine, was assassinated by native employees. Within a few weeks every mine in the country, except one, was deserted."

The *Arizona Citizen* of Jan. 7, 1871 said the "celebrated Cerro Colorado mine situated 70 miles south of Tucson is one of great

extent and richness and yesterday a miner from there exhibited a specimen of very rich silver ore with ruby tinge, which he says comes from the vein about one mile from the Cerro Colorado shaft. This new discovery is being worked to advantage on a limited scale. . . ."

According to historians, Charles D. Poston, who organized the Sonora Exploring and Mining Co. in 1865, secured title to mines including the Cerro Colorado when there were 29 silver mines. The Heintzelman mine, named for Samuel P. Heintzelman, president of the mining company, was the most famous.

The story in the **Hartford Evening Press** noted it was not the plans of the superintendent of the mine (apparently the Cerro Colorado-Heintzelman) to "rely on one shaft alone but to sink at short intervals on the whole extent of the vein which has been traced for over two miles . . . to rely on a hundred working shafts on this and other veins. . . ."

After the Civil War, miners returned and by 1879 a post office was established here. The mine remained active many years.

Recently, after first taking off on two wrong dirt roads about seven or eight miles out of Arivaca, the writer found the site of the former mining town.

Mrs. Dean Mitchell of Tucson, a student in a Pima College class on "Ghost Towns," and her family were on the scene absorbing the yesteryear atmosphere. She reported she had seen three mine shafts. Still another visitor spotted a mine shaft near the trail into the area.

Elisa Lujan and her husband, Juan, live in a trailer at the history-steeped site, Mrs. Lujan, who has lived here since 1964, confirmed the adobe walls were remains of Cerro Colorado.

And, sure enough, looming ahead was the conical red hill, the Cerro Colorado (red mountain) the landmark for which the area was named.

Mrs. Lujan discredited the idea of a mass grave for miners killed in a cave-in. She said their bodies were never recovered. She did say, however, that "up around a little trail there is an old grave."

The wind was blowing cold, the bare mesquite limbs quivering in frenzy. Word of the grave triggered a detour beyond those adobe walls.

Mostly, Cerro Colorado's souvenir past lives on in memories.

CHARLESTON
above the San Pedro

A bonanza in adobe, crumbling in odd shapes and dimensions, marks this ghost town asleep on the west bank of the San Pedro River.

Adobe ruins peak through the jungle of mesquite, paloverde and thornbrush enveloping the old town that long ago milled silver ore from the Tombstone mines.

The wind, roaring in gusts up to 45 mph during this reporter's visit there, deepened the eerie fascination of the haunting ground adventure. Ghost town fanciers waded the meandering San Pedro to discover the souvenir town.

Faint paths criss-crossed the maze of snagging mesquite and ancient adobes, some with windows sagging in emptiness. Piles of weathered lumber spoke of collapsed cabins. And elsewhere the ashes of a campfire with beer cans was a modern day note.

In the west part of the deserted village, 40 foot bluffs dropped to the river below.

The bizarre place is located three-fourths mile downstream from the San Pedro bridge on the old Charleston Road between

Visitors wade San Pedro to reach ghost town Charleston.

A ghost town fancier peeks through old adobe.

Tombstone and Sierra Vista.

The quiet today seems hard to equate with the area's lively past. Before Charleston went into eternal sleep, induced by the flooding of the mines in Tombstone in the mid 1880s, its population of several hundred had carved a colorful niche in early Arizona history.

Charleston was laid out in 1878-79. Along its Main Street were mercantile stores, a restaurant and, as could be expected, an ample number of saloons. One scribe wrote there were also "naughty girls." The river camp, smaller than Tombstone, was described by historians as a center for rustlers and soldiers from Fort Huachuca.

It was founded because Tombstone had no water to work reduction facilities for its mines. The San Pedro River, then much narrower, was a constant source of water for the mills.

Most anything could—and did—happen here, including a time when barroom celebrants invaded a church service. While cautious parishoners left, the minister was forced to stay and preach a sermon.

The legend says that a healthy contribution was made when the collection plate was passed, but nonetheless, one celebrant was later fined for disturbing the peace.

So, as one can see, there was an arbitrary brand of justice.

And, commentators of the frontier scene noted that Charleston had facilities for a prosperous town and its existence was not entirely dependent on the mining interests.

Time marched on with its inexorable toll, and when the mills closed (the mines were flooded in Tombstone) residents started moving away. The desertion eventually brought death to the community.

The old town knew a rash of activity during World War II, when it was used for war games by soldiers from Fort Huachuca.

COCHISE
friendliness and tranquility

Arizona travelers with a hankering to sample a different lifestyle will find this remote village, born in Old West history, a novel interlude.

There's an 1892 hotel, laden with antiques, that offers overnight guests a glimpse into bygone times.

Not far away there's a general store that opened in 1913, still the town's meeting place.

And like most old Western towns, Cochise has its share of venerable residents who like to reminisce about the old days, giving the listener that peek into history.

Cochise is named for the famed Chiricahua Apache chief. It is nestled four miles south of Interstate 10, west of Willcox. It is an idyllic setting, where the pace is slow and where nobody keeps tabs on the population figures.

Rex Brown, 70, sat at a round table in the Cochise General Store, nursing a brew. He talked about the "beautiful" life in the old town he has called home since 1911.

"I can sit in my front yard under the trees and talk to the birds. There are rabbits, quail, even snakes. But it's the friendliness of the people, the tranquility."

It was near noon and Judith Berreau, the general store's owner, kept an anxious eye on the clock. It would soon be time for the Arizona Electric Power Co. work crew to head in for lunch.

The menu listed a beef "san" for a buck, a ham sandwich for $1.10. A large bowl of chili went for 95 cents.

The community dates back to the establishment of a railroad station in 1887. Cochise was once the junction of the Southern Pacific and Arizona Eastern railroads, and served as shipping point for the old Pearce mines.

In a way, it was the railroad that spawned the Cochise Hotel.

Lillie Harrington, the hotel manager, said the town's first telegrapher started the hotel figuring that folks who got off at the station should have a place to stay.

The hotel opened only with beds and rooms but the "new" addition, the dining hall, came along in 1896. Still, it is no ordinary hostelry.

"You can't just walk in off the street and come in for dinner and a night's lodging," Mrs. Harrington said. "There must be advance reservations. I only cook steak and chicken dinners. It would not be profitable if I cooked a bunch of food and no one showed up."

Owned by Mrs. Thomas B. Husband, the hotel has been placed

Cochise Hotel dates back to 1890's.

on the National Register of Historical Places by the U.S. Interior Department. An old Seth Thomas "backwinder" clock ticks away on the kitchen wall. There are large, old tables in the dining room, a marble-topped sideboard, charming chandeliers, an ancient high-chair.

An oak wardrobe, almost ceiling high, with large panels of plate-glass mirror, adorns the parlor with its velvet sofas. Each bedroom and suite had its own toilet although there are pitchers and bowls for atmosphere.

Mrs. Harrington, a lively 71, brusque yet friendly, pointed out there is no air conditioning in the summer, but the thick adobe walls provide protection from the summer heat.

"I can sleep up to 11 in the hotel. There's no liquor served here, but some people bring their own," she said, pointing to strings of empty bottles used for outside decor.

"When the weather is cooler there are more guests. They come in from Tucson, Phoenix, El Paso and Sun City," she said.

There is an elementary school with Tim Hart, 35, the head teacher, coach and bus driver. Hart's grandfather also taught in the school.

A 95-year-old resident remembered the time when residents armed themselves with rifles when they heard Pancho Villa and his gang were headed toward Cochise. The feared visit never material-ized, the resident said.

CONTENTION CITY
death at an early age

Windswept remains of the mill camp that was conceived and died in less than a decade in the nineteenth century can scarcely be classed a ghost town.

There's only a desolate trace of the community that pulsated from three mills for the Tombstone mine ores before going into eternal sleep. The town has literally given up the ghost.

Hardy souls, willing to wade the cold San Pedro River, some three miles north of Fairbank, can gain the portals. And, it was learned since, there is a road in from the other side of the river. Even then, the crumbling adobe walls are reached by searching, climbing, the catclaw bushes snagging the clothing of intruders. *(Advice: if the weather is wet, stay away.)*

On a wintertime visit here, a cottonwood tree, bereft of its foliage, spread gaunt limbs above the rippling San Pedro. Above and beyond eroded banks, part of an old mill loomed formidably.

It's hard to conceive today that business was once bustling at the Dewdrop and Headlight saloons. Or, that the three mills, the Grand Central, Head Center and the Contention, provided the livelihood

The desert closes in on crumbling Contention.

Not much remains at Contention City.

for a peak population of 200.

In 1879, within a week after the town had been surveyed, the sale of lots was underway and building preparations launched.

About that time ten American women steamed into the rugged isolated camp to brave life there with their husbands. Stage lines plied from Tombstone and Tucson with daily stops here. A stage line was later purchased by "Sandy Bob" Crouch, an uncle of a Glendale man. A post office was established in 1880.

Actually life in the community belied its name.

There was no more contention here than in any other frontier town. Contention, apparently was so named because it milled the ore from the great Contention Mine. Still, some historians state that the mine was so named because of a claim dispute.

The camp's demise came about when Tombstone mines closed because of flooding and the mills shut down. The post office was discontinued in 1888.

On a hill on the east side of the river, between Contention and Fairbank, is the old cemetery with some crosses and fences still around.

COURTLAND
"will eventually be the county seat"

Bleak and desolate are the words for the scene at this old mining town—ruins of the jail house and store buildings with windows that gape in nothingness and, somewhere in the hills, the mines that spawned the place.

Yet the historical vibes are good. It was once a booming mining camp pulsating with people and the usual accoutrements of a lifestyle befitting the age and purpose of the frontier community.

Courtland had a newspaper—*The Courtland Arizonan*, established in February, 1909, and published every Sunday.

The town even had a baseball team.

In fact in April, 1909, the *Arizonan* discussed the town baseball nine's coming season as promising to be a "hot one." It added that the team manager Hazard (not bothering with the first name) "is going to spring something good."

On another subject, the paper noted that Courtland "is growing rapidly, the railroads will soon be unloading freight in the city limits and then the population will grow by leaps and bounds.

"That Courtland will eventually be the county seat of Cochise County is just as certain as its destiny as the population and commercial center of the county," the paper waxed on.

Old files at the Arizona Historical Society indicate that Courtland received its name from Courtland Young, one of the owners of the Great Western Mining Co. Courtland, established around 1909, was considered to be one of the most promising copper camps in Arizona. Four large mining companies were working in the area since surface conditions indicated the presence of a copper bonanza.

In the vagaries of mining, the boom waned. But, it wasn't until 1942 that the post office was closed. As late as 1968, a newspaper reported that the hills around Courtland were still rich in ore and that leaseholders there were active.

In June, 1959, a wire service story datelined Courtland, said a ghost here had been caught after only two months in operation.

The ghost had been described as "white, shooting out sparks and screaming like a cat at midnight Saturdays when it jumped out of a mine shaft at people."

A distraught woman hired a Tucson detective agency to dig into the mystery. In the end, the ghost proved to be a 55-year-old local citizen dressed in a sheet to scare his three teenagers into coming home before midnight on Saturdays.

Courtland is located on a dusty, unnumbered road between

A picture window view at ghost town Courtland

Pearce and Gleeson in southern Arizona. On a previous trip through here the writer refrained from sightseeing around the old store—for good reason. A sign warned of bad consequences for anyone caught trespassing. The sign is gone, the store owner dead and buried in the Gleeson cemetery.

While Courtland's demise is total and no one lives here, we did find a living creature—a little calf—lying quietly beneath a bush. Just as we wondered if the calf were injured and what to do about it, a cow in the area emitted a loud bawl. The calf jumped to its feet and took off.

In nearby Gleeson, we heard an unusual story that may explain why the old store building here was stripped so thoroughly. It seems the owner sold the property for an enormous sum, but after his death there was accounting for only a fraction of the amount.

The silence in Courtland now is complete—save for a mother cow and her gamboling calf or an occasional motorist stopping to wield a camera.

And yet—there's somehow another sound—a plaintive refrain echoing in the hills as relentless time and weather and even people close the gap on Courtland's past.

CRITTENDEN
population: one

Crittenden, a ghost town, nestled in the quiet beauty of the Canelo Hills near Patagonia, boasts one ancient house and cemetery of matching vintage.

Its population is one—Mrs. Helene May, born 74 years ago in Crittenden during its bustling heyday.

The settlement, known as early as 1860 as Casa Blanca, was later named Crittenden. Mrs. May's father, John Smith, arrived there around 1880 and was responsible for securing the rail depot and ore platform. The hamlet became an important rail shipping point for lead, copper and silver from such mines as the World's Fair and the rich Hermosa.

Crittenden is approximately four miles south of Fort Crittenden along the Sonoita-Patagonia highway.

Mule and horse teams, sometimes numbering 36 animals, hauled the ore from area mines to the Crittenden rail point. Noisy drivers and teams arrived day and night, and there was also the military traffic to Ft. Crittenden.

It was logical that in 1885 Smith built a hotel. The two-story rock building, which is Mrs. May's home today, became a mecca for travelers and teamsters.

As a small girl, Helene kept the chimneys of the coal oil lamps clean and shining, and by the age of nine she was baking the bread for the hardy roomers. Fifty cents paid for more deluxe downstairs accommodations, while 25 cents drew a cot with fresh sheets on the upper floor.

"Fifty cent meals were prepared from garden fresh vegetables and meat bought from ranchers," Mrs. May recalled. "Big cakes of ice wrapped in blankets came by rail from Nogales. On Sundays, the summertime treat was sometimes ice cream.

"Meals were served family style until some of the teamsters got to taking six eggs at a time from the platter. Then mother started serving plate dinners."

Coffee was served from handleless mugs, weighing a pound each. A few survived the hotel days, and are prized souvenirs. "A well-aimed mug could keep hotel guests in line," Mrs. May remembered.

In time, mining operations waned and were moved elsewhere. So did the population. Around the turn of the century, most residents

Crittenden native Helene May displays hotel mug which kept guests "in line."

had dismantled their homes and moved.

In 1887 an earthquake cracked the upper story of the hotel from the peak to the keystone of the ground floor door. The top story was removed, but the surviving building is staunch.

The house has been home for all but one year for Mrs. May. Its four-way roof, white picket fence and nearby lofty windmill are familiar sights along Highway 82.

Her stories of the old days are legion.

There was the time the Indians murdered a mailman. "They riddled his mail sack and stole his wagon and horse," she recounted.

Five fierce dogs and two cats provide protection and company for the pioneer.

DOS CABEZAS
the old adobe lifestyle

Wild spring flowers carpeted the dirt floor here of a roofless building, its old adobe walls washed in sunshine along main street.

And beyond the thoroughfare, a fragment of a stagecoach stop complete with rusting black safe is an eye-catcher. Elsewhere is a three-wall skeleton of a schoolhouse said to be the first school in Cochise County.

For lovers of Arizona history, the place is a real Mother Lode.

Yet, Dos Cabezas, some 14 miles south of Willcox on State 186 is all too often overlooked by motorists hastening on to the "Wonderland of Rocks" in the Chiricahuas.

If Dos Cabezas can be classed a ghost town, it's a lively one. With a population "guess-timated" at 30, the place can not be relegated entirely to the past.

Although there are no gasoline and food facilities here, Dos Cabezas has one shop—the Dos Cabezas Crafts Center, operated by Paul and Mary Duncan. And, elsewhere, Pete and Carol Brunner, a young couple busy restoring a two-story house here, create attractive art in stained glass. Another resident creates wood carvings.

Gold and silver mines in 1878 launched the place although it was in existence long before. Dos Cabezas was named for two bald summits. The place was first called Ewell Springs, a half-mile east of the town. In the 1880's there were some 300 living here.

A reporter in 1881 described the place as a "cozy, sunny nook." He said the locale would be picturesque if liberally supplied with trees and running water. All over the peaks and hills are heaps of rock, marking the boundary of some hoped for bonanza, the scribe noted.

"This morning, your correspondent took a stroll and climbed to the top of one of the highest peaks," the scribe continued. "Far below lay the little town. There are upwards of 50 buildings, mostly adobe. The town has one hotel—not first class, three saloons, blacksmith shop, a post office, stamp mill for gold ore and several arrastras (a device formerly used for crushing ore) worked by private individuals."

Among rich mines on the gold-bearing ledge near the Dos Cabezas peaks, according to the story, were the Silver Cave, Greenhorn and Murphy. Shafts had been sunk to 100 feet.

Today, a sign at the stagecoach stop says "Butterfield Stage," but *Arizona Place Names* says the stage station was created by the Birch Route in 1857. In 1971 Ben Anderson, then a Dos Cabezas

resident, said it was here that pony express riders stopped to change mounts enroute from El Paso to Tucson.

Anderson, who arrived with his family here by covered wagon in 1911, said drought in 1916 brought downfall to the community. "The cattle died, wells went dry and mines started shutting down. Most were closed by 1926," he told this reporter.

The Duncans spent their professional lives in Chicago, Paul as a mechanical engineer, she as an executive secretary with Kraft. They believe their shop is in a building once used as a hospitality house by the manager of The Mascot Mine.

The Duncans, residents here since 1968, enjoy their Dos Cabezas lifestyle.

"It's the serenity, the peacefulness, the ability to be ourselves," she explained. "We get satisfaction out of teaching and feel we are giving something back to the community."

The Brunners with their two sons enjoy restoring the frame house that belonged to her grandfather.

Vintage Dos Cabezas in a pretty corner of southeastern Arizona is well worth a visit. The crumbling, souvenir-old adobes are losing their grip on the past.

FAIRBANK
the train doesn't stop anymore

This historic village along the San Pedro River had a population of three on Jan. 2, 1971. But, the next day an old house, a former stage stop station, was rented and the population tripled.

Miss Charlotte Blank, postmaster and owner-operator of the store here, was busy at her duties behind the antique wire postal cage that had been here since 1882. The relic store building's adobe walls were a novel 21 inches thick. The post office was established May 16, 1883.

The old depot is gone, but a Southern Pacific freight train lumbered through here daily—without stopping.

Otherwise the town named for N. K. Fairbank, an official with the Grand Central Mining Co., rests quietly.

The place blossomed with the arrival of the railroad around 1882 and in time became a shipping center for ore and cattle.

Supplies at the old Fairbank Mercantile Store were all but nil.

Former stage stop at Fairbank

The friendly Miss Blank said she wasn't "bothering now" with the store, save to sell off remnants of merchandise and furnishings.

A short while back hunters and passersby could stop at the store for a can of beer and a visit around the old table near the pot-bellied stove. Miss Blank said she had quit the beer business, however.

Republic files reveal the community suffered milestone events like the September night in 1890 when the San Pedro River went on a rampage, flooding over its banks. There were many narrow escapes and much loss of property.

Of course there was the daily arrival of the trains to create interest in the early days, even a train robbery in the late 1880s.

The town had the usual businesses including three restaurants, five saloons, a hotel and a jail with a swinging door. During our visit, iron bars on a window in back of the store still marked the jail area.

Elsewhere in the old townsite, leased by a cattle company, undergrowth is closing. But, at Miss Blank's house, shared with a friend, a white and red picket fence puts up a neat front.

Fairbank is on State 82, about 10 miles out of Tombstone. (On a recent stop in Fairbank, the old store was behind a locked gate.)

FORT BOWIE
protection from Geronimo

The wind blew a gentle gale up Apache Pass toward the remains of this historic fort.

The adobe walls were placid, serene, but the Stars and Stripes whipped and snapped in the morning breeze.

Ghost town and history fans walk 1½ miles to get to the fort, built in the Chiricahuas in 1868, by climbing up and down hills and gullies and Syphon Canyon.

Visitors leave their cars after traveling routes from either Willcox or Bowie. A well-defined path coils past Fort Bowie cemetery, the old Butterfield Stage stop, Apache Spring where conflict centered a century ago between Apaches and Anglos, and two benches for tired hikers.

Visitors may putter on a path through the maze of ruins, each marked for such places as the cavalry barracks, school, infantry kitchen, butcher shop, telegraph office.

One of the largest buildings was the Post Trader, where the fort's women did their domestic shopping. In other rooms officers could play billiards and drink.

Apart, but nearby, are remains of the first fort that was built in 1862.

Shortly after Geronimo's final surrender in 1886, Fort Bowie's

From one old historic wall to another

Only weather-worn walls stand at fort's cavalry barracks.

life as a military post ended. For awhile it lingered on, benefiting little more than the local economy. On Oct. 17, 1894, the fort officially was abandoned. The garrison flag with 44 stars was lowered for the last time.

The 118-man garrison of the Second Cavalry troopers, accompanied by nine women and children, rode down to Bowie Station and boarded a train for their new post at Fort Logan, Colorado.

In June, 1911, fort lands were sold at public auction for $1.25 to $2.50 an acre. The fort's wooden timbers immediately were salvaged to build ranch buildings.

Finally on Aug. 30, 1964, Fort Bowie National Historic Site was authorized by Congress to be administered by the National Park Service, Department of the Interior.

Visitors can buy colored slides and postcards and historical books about the fort at the ranger station.

Rangers list a few precautions for the trail. Beware of rattlesnakes, water in the washes, loose gravel on the trail. There also is the advisability of carrying drinking water. A recent roundtrip hike plus inspection of the fort required more than three hours.

WAGON TRAIN
MASSACRE SITE
1861

Massacre site beside dirt road to Ft. Bowie

FORT CRITTENDEN
Call it "camp" or "fort,"
Its life was short!

The wind whipped the mesquite limbs into a frenzied dance about old adobe walls melting into the ground from which they came. But the eeriness of the setting seemed somehow fitting.

Fort Crittenden had died here 100 years ago. And the intervening century had taken its toll.

Once cavalry units were hurriedly dispatched from the camp that was inaugurated during war against Apaches under Cochise. In quieter times, however, the men in the remoteness must have found time heavy on their hands. The camp's tiny place in the pages of Arizona history dated only from 1867 to 1873.

Arizona Place Names and a book, *Frontier Military Posts of Arizona* refer to the military installation as "fort." However, a letter in the Arizona Historical Society files from the War Department Adjutant General's Office, Washington, dated Jan.' 29, 1926, referred to the place as "camp." It quoted a military order from the Department of California that the new camp in the Sonoita Valley east of Tubac "be known as Camp Crittenden."

The first tents at the place gave way to buildings of adobe, wood slats and even earth roofs. The guardhouse had a more substantial core, and in time there was even a 12-bed hospital.

Located between Santa Cruz County's Patagonia and Sonoita on 111

state Route 82, the camp remnant is heralded by a small marker. Recent visitors paused to read the sign, then casually scanned the horizon. There was a big surprise. Adobe walls in the distance peeked among the brush and trees.

Turning on a ranch road, motorists were confronted with a "No Trespassing" sign. Backing out in compliance, they were heartened to see a ranch car approaching. The driver verified the ruins were of Old Camp Crittenden and gave permission for a close-up look.

Promising to stay on the trail, the visitors proceeded with care and mounting interest. It was somehow akin to finding a treasure, visiting the ruins perched on a gentle rise in the lush ranch country.

There were unexplainable sinks and adobe walls still clutching the earth with dogged tenacity. Historians note that water for the camp was from springs and two wells within the garrison.

Soldiers are said to have played baseball for recreation and exercised on parallel bars. One account notes that drinking alcohol was a severe problem at the lonely outpost.

Arizona Place Names records that Ft. Crittenden was abandoned because of "unhealthy conditions," but does not elaborate.

Some historians speculated that military attention shifted elsewhere after Indian Chief Cochise surrendered. Later, in June 1872, a newspaper noted that men were breaking camp.

Camp Crittenden's days were over. No one, apparently, mourned its demise.

GLEESON
a return to former haunts

Motorists bouncing over a graveled road to Gleeson can easily slip into the mood to sample its ghost town aura.

Travelers may well know that the copper and turquoise mines that once boomed the place have shut down. The post office closed in 1939, and melting adobes add color and atmosphere. All this, yet a few lively spirits (population less than 10) call this place home.

The 16-mile stretch of roads and washes from Tombstone winds through mountains and desert, and on a recent trip only two cars were encountered. Few other roads in Arizona have a roadside sign that says, "Private land—cattle have right of way."

A stiff wind bounced the creosote and mesquite bushes, and roadside flowers—purple, white and yellow—danced frantically. Dust sifted in the vehicle despite closed windows and air conditioning.

From a distance, a tall concrete archway loomed commandingly in Gleeson. A closeup look confirmed the suspicion—the once elegant entranceway goes nowhere. And, in a surprising twist, a little black dog came from the midst of the foundation rubble to bark shrilly at visitors.

The burned-out jail stands naked, and someone with no yen for things historical has destroyed the old oak hanging tree. Old adobe walls pop up in sundry places, the biggest being the four walls of the early-day hospital.

On a hillside an old cemetery, dotted with ornate grave markers and fences, is the resting place for many key residents of earlier Gleeson.

Mining of turquoise gave the place its first name, and the post office from 1890 to 1894 was so named. Later, John Gleeson mined here and by 1900, the new post office opened by that name.

The town suffered a devastating fire in 1912. An old newspaper clipping at the Arizona Historical Society dated June 8, 1912, described the $100,000 fire. It seems Deputy W. W. Gales, making his rounds before retiring for the night, noticed smoke issuing from a warehouse owned by B. A. Taylor, and gave the alarm by firing five shots as he ran to the building.

The fire spread rapidly taking every building in the block on both sides of the street. Some people, in view of the rapidity with which the fire spread, were confident that "oil had been used and the match applied at different places."

Paramount Pictures brought in a large entourage for the filming of "The Mysterious Rider," an adaptation of Zane Grey's novel. Some say this occurred in 1933, others in the 1940s.

The town backgrounded with mine-pocked mountainsides died after copper mining operations shut down. One resident placed this date in 1957, another about 1964.

Willard and Shirley Mayfield came here from Tombstone 20 years ago. They have closed their museum there that featured old bottles and other artifacts. Now, they enjoy the quiet place from the vantage point of their trailer home, complete with television and phone.

"I wouldn't trade this place for any I've ever lived in," Mrs. Mayfield said. "No one could pay me to go someplace else. We like the climate, the quietness, the good air."

Mayfield said there's still a little gold mining going on.

The old store building was closed for business during a recent visit. But the curious—those seeking a bit of ghost town lore—still visit the place.

Roy Woodruff, a retiree, lives in his small trailer beneath a spreading oak tree.

"It's a little bit too quiet, but I'd rather live here than in town," he said. "At night I watch television or listen to my radio. I can get Berlin."

Maria Queroz Martinez was born in Gleeson in 1912. She attended the local school, and after her marriage lived a while in Phoenix, Benson and Tombstone. She returned here to stay in 1940, living with a son in a house that belonged to her mother. One son worked in the Shannon Copper Mine here.

One of the showpieces about the ghost town is a sign that says "Gleeson, Az." Mayfield made the overhead sign of bottle necks against a wire fence background.

"There has been a million pictures made of that sign," Woodruff quipped, as a reporter backed off to add one more snap to the total.

THE GHOST TRAIL
Marcos de Niza slept here

A little known backwoods road slithers along near the international border between Arizona and Mexico. Some call it "The Ghost Trail."

And, although mostly graveled, the trail is paved with Arizona history. And eye-catching scenery.

Motorists who like to mix adventure with their travel will relish the trail that weaves in shades of Coronado's Expedition, old mines that flourished long ago, mining camp remnants and a quaint border station.

There's much more—the colorful Coronado National Forest, towering mountains, cattle grazing country, unusual flora, a peaceful valley. The solitude of the little trafficked road is a big plus.

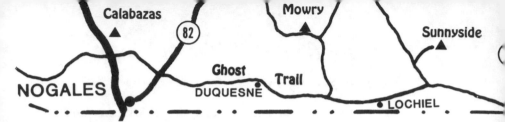

The starting point is Nogales, a unique border town.

It's fun to preface the Ghost Trail with an overnight stay in Nogales, Arizona, arriving in time for an afternoon sashay across the border to Nogales, Sonora, Mexico. Browsing in the maze of shops is a fringe benefit.

Next morning, get an early start on the trail, making sure supplies of gasoline, water and food are ample. The trip from Nogales to Sierra Vista is around 80 miles.

Nose off State 82 at a red school house and hug to the little trail eastward, zeroed ahead for Duquesne. The road beckons invitingly, especially for travelers jaded by bumper-to-bumper traffic or metropolitan areas. The somnolence of the old trail offers a quiet panacea.

The graveled road, sometimes arched by old shade, glides by old ranches, cud-chewing cattle and green terrain backgrounded by purple-hued mountains.

At times the road is washboardy and narrow, verging by wild flowers, huge mesquite and walnut trees. Gray squirrels dash across the road and lucky motorists may see a roadrunner. Signs along the road should be closely observed to keep on the right trail.

At a crest in the Patagonia Mountains in the Coronado National Forest, Nogales, some 15 miles in the distance, appears sprawled against hilly moorings. Travelers park their cars to savor the panorama and call of wild birds.

On the other side of the mountains, the trail scene changes and veers into mining area. A loop off the main trail takes motorists into Duquesne and the area of the Bonanza and Nash Mines. Washington Camp and Duquesne were closely allied in the 1880s and 1890s. There are other mines in the area.

Back on the main trail again, San Rafael Valley offers a charming change of pace with its old windmills, rustic corrals and ranch homes.

A chapter in history unfolds in an unexpected scene—a huge concrete cross. The historical marker memorializes Fray Marcos de Niza, "the first European west of the Rockies." The roadside cross complete with benches marks the spot where Fray Marcos, as delegate of the viceroy in Mexico, crossed the border on April 12, 1539.

At Lochiel, a little used international gateway, Mrs. Helen Mills has served as U.S. Customs Inspector many years.

The quiet border village, at times with a population of 12, is

Historical marker memorializes Fray Marcos de Niza, "the first European west of the Rockies."

separated from Mexico by a chain link and wire fence. Traffic at the border point is small, but still it is an international check point. Mrs. Mills once checked a van crossing the border and found it contained 365 pounds of marijuana.

Mrs. Mills, whose husband works in the area, finds the isolation "tranquil rather than lonely."

The trail out of Lochiel coasted miles and miles through rangeland with views of the Huachuca Mountains. One ranch is said to be the site of a John Wayne movie.

Gaining altitude again, the road in the Coronado National Forest narrows, passing through little canyons, small bridges and streams. Junipers and oak spiced the scenery and at 6,300 ft., Montezuma Pass, some 55 miles from Nogales, is achieved. The location offers sweeping vistas of San Rafael and San Pedro Valleys and Mexico.

The Coronado National Memorial commemorates the historic march of Francisco Vasquez de Coronado and symbolizes the importance of the Spanish in the history and culture of the southwest.

At the pass, the Coronado Peak Trail challenges the hardy to climb a foot trail flanked with stakes denoting such varied flora as bear grass, emery, oak, lichen and mosses, alligator juniper, mountain yucca, Mexican pinon.

Back in the car, motorists find the trail drops drastically eastward, the ribbon road twisting and turning. For some the descent is a little hair-raising, and drivers must take special care. The road finally drops into a delightful picnic area.

Eventually the trail fades into Arizona 92. Travelers may continue east to Naco and Bisbee or north to Sierra Vista or Tombstone.

The rugged trail laced with history stands tall among travel memories.

GREATERVILLE
great for picnicking

Four families or some 25 people comprised the population of Greaterville in 1965. The quiet settlement, a reminder of more glorious days, is located four miles off Highway 83 along a graveled road which juts away about eight miles north of Sonoita.

A tiny sign pointed to the village, where the water supply was raised bucket by bucket from an old well. A school girl beside the well said she panned gold for recreation.

History records that after the discovery of placer gold in the area in 1874, miners rushed to the location and the town of Greaterville developed. The mining district was organized March 17, 1875, and an old mine is still visible in the area.

Arizona Place Names says the project was plagued by lack of water. Placers were worked by rockers and long tom (a trough for washing gold bearing earth), and, indicating the hardship, water was brought in canvas or goatskin bags from Gardner Canyon four miles away.

Miners began to desert the camp in 1881 when gold played out. Still others left because of Indian attacks. The community enjoyed a brief revival in 1900 when a hydraulic plant was installed in nearby Kentucky Gulch.

Some men entered the camp via Renegade Pass trying to avoid the law on their way from the border.

Four-wheel-drive travelers may enjoy a mountainous trail out of Greaterville through oak, cedar, pine and manzanita country. The trail crosses Ophir Gulch, spirals and finally eases to a foot trail on the crest of the Santa Ritas. The sylvan beauty and quiet provide a great picnic setting.

Greaterville's water supply

HILLTOP
spirits of a heyday

This ghost town is aptly named. It's near the top of a mountain, reached by a tortuous four-wheel drive trail and a brief hike.

Rewards for history buffs are ample, but there is little left of the things that once made this place bustle.

On a windblown day in Hilltop east—Hilltop comes in two parts —old metal whipped and squeaked in the breeze. And, a wood gate, slate grey in age with rusting nails, continued to swing open and shut as though propelled by some unseen hand.

Put them all together—the wind, the spooky sound effects, the sights—and they add up to a scenario proper for things ghostly.

Elsewhere, probably in the residential section, there was a miscellany in concrete floors of buildings long gone. And, simply wondrous on a May day, there were wild rose bushes with red blooms in delicate fragrance.

The rubble was king size—sprawling old lumber with sharp nails, sheet metal, rusting machinery. Visitors stepped warily avoiding places that might collapse—like a flight of wooden stairs that go no place in particular.

The old divided Hilltop mining camp was linked by a tunnel, no longer safe, which this reporter did not find.

Hilltop on the east side of the mountain is reached by the road to Portal, out of San Simon, then a right turn into the Chiricahuas on

Old stairway to no place at ghost town Hilltop

Rusting machinery at Hilltop mine scene

the White Tail Canyon Road.

It is best to inquire along the way as a left fork in the road veers into the camp—finally. Several residents live in lower recesses of the Hilltop area.

This reporter talked to two residents along the trail and obtained consent to enter the place. Warnings were issued about the unsafe place.

Bob Fagan, a retired teacher, put us on the right track, but we did not find the foundation of the school house with desks.

In a higher area of Hilltop, an old mine headgate loomed in age, and elsewhere was the old mine. Both are places to keep a safe distance away.

History records that the original strike at Hilltop was made on the west side of the main mountain ridge by Jack Dunn in the early 1880s. The early settlement was known as Ayers Camp. Brothers Frank and John Hand acquired the property in the 1890s. Ensuing events saw development of active mining on the northeast slope of the mountain.

It was in 1917 that the tunnel was driven through the mountain to the northeast. A new and larger camp developed on the eastern side.

Historians agree that it was in 1913 when the Hilltop Metals Mining Co. entered the picture. Hilltop had a post office from 1920 to 1945. The mines may have produced lead and zinc although one historical account mentioned the impact of fluctuating price of silver on the mine. The 1930 population hovered at 100.

Anyway, as in the case of most mining camps, Hilltop served its purpose, then bowed from the active scene.

In fact, it died.

MOWRY
dangerous mine shafts

A breeze stirred the branches of a scrub oak tree and sifted on through the gaping window of a crumbling adobe house.

Dangling metal creaked eerily. A large squirrel perched ever so fleetingly on a vacant window sill. Even that wispy commotion was a bit disquieting in a place so long "ghostly."

But later there was new life. A couple cruised by on a motorcycle and motorists in a compact car halted, a cloud of pinkish dust in their wake.

The little lane twisting through the old mining camp was flanked with assorted adobe skeletons. A frame building and sundry wood porches had already given up the ghost, so to speak, sagging in the collapse. Walls in assorted shapes and silhouettes stood in stark nakedness.

Mowry's heyday died long ago, but remains of old mines are ghastly.

In Patagonia, an oldtimer advised about the old buildings. "But beware of the open mine shafts," he said. "One drops 250 feet."

The advice proved in order. The shafts are indeed hazardous and there are several in and around the area.

Historically, the old Patagonia mine site was purchased in 1859 by Lt. Sylvester Mowry who promptly changed the name to his own.

The roof leaks, but the picture window view is great.

He employed over 100 men and shipped out $1.5 million in ore.

According to *Arizona Place Names,* Mowry was seized in June 1862, as a southern sympathizer and imprisoned about six months. He was discharged, the opinion of the court being there was no evidence against him to prove he actively supported the Confederacy.

The Patagonia Mine, historians say, is an old mine but was rediscovered in 1858 by a Mexican herder, who sold it for a pony and several articles of little value to army officers at Fort Crittenden. They finally sold the mine to Mowry.

Mowry, history records, became a tireless worker for the advancement of Arizona. He was elected to Congress in 1857 and 1858. Congress, however, refused to seat him because Arizona was not yet a territory.

The mining camp area about 13 miles southeast of Patagonia is in the Coronado National Forest.

We did not find the cemetery. It is said that of the 17 men buried there, 15 died violently.

Old adobe home at Oro Blanco

ORO BLANCO
a place to remember

Quiet beauty and history blend in this remote area of the Coronado National Forest a few miles north of the Arizona-Mexico border.

On a leisurely tour there, bird watchers lined the bank of Oro Blanco Creek, field glasses poised for sighting.

On the other side of the rushing stream, sightseers, hunting for the ghost town of Oro Blanco, paused for a picnic.

The Carl Widups of Tucson relaxed on a log for a lunch break. Newly married after a 41-year separation, the couple were there to try their hands at gold panning.

Occasionally, other vehicles splashed through the creek's path on the road. Dave Keener, watchman on the Oro Blanco Noon Ranch, drove by observingly.

The Oro Blanco area, some seven miles from Arivaca, is reached over a hilly road with washes.

It was in April, 1879, nearly 100 years ago, that Dr. Adolphus Noon, who had served with the Union forces in the Civil War, chose to settle in the area. His first home was near the Oro Blanco Creek wash, where a corral stands nearby today.

The only doctor in the mining and rangeland area, his patients sometimes paid him with a cow or a heifer. In fact, according to his grandson, Horton Noon, now of Nogales, this was how the long-ago doctor started in ranching.

The Noon family, which has been there since, became widely known as ranchers in Southern Arizona.

Up the road about a half-mile beyond the creek are old adobe buildings that once housed the Oro Blanco stage station, a guest house and quarters for a Chinese cook.

The adobes were built around 1885, Noon said. Nearby is the Oro Blanco Dam Lake, built 25 to 30 years ago, shimmering and deep in some areas.

The stage station is not at the original town of Oro Blanco, which came into being when there was activity on a vein of gold-bearing ore where work originated in the unknown past. According to *Arizona Place Names,* mining was resumed in 1873. Of interest, too, the mine lay so close to the International Boundary that a survey was made to be sure it was in Arizona.

The mines are about 2½ miles in the hills south and east from the stage station, with the Austerlitz mine near the roadway at Warsaw Wash.

A post office, established in Oro Blanco in 1879, was discontinued in April, 1915.

The mines and the adobe buildings belong to the Noon Ranch.

Noon is refurbishing and restoring the old adobe buildings. A third generation of the founding Noon, he is preserving the buildings for a newer generation of the family, he said.

The main adobe building, including four bedrooms, each with a fireplace, is surrounded with peach, apple and elderberry trees. Spreading mesquite trees on one side the building remain trimmed and preserved for a sentimental reason.

It was there that Noon's father, Arthur Noon, leashed his horses while he courted the area school teacher, Martha Clayton, who lived in the adobe structure. The two later married.

Keener pointed to the old cemetery. Its tall white crosses on a windswept knoll can be seen from a distance.

The trek to the cemetery was well worthwhile. The bare mesquite tree limbs danced madly in the March wind. About 50 graves are in the old resting place.

The newer Oro Blanco before the turn of the century did have its social side.

An article in the *Weekly Arizona Enterprise,* Florence, Jan. 3,

Oro Blanco cemetery on wind-swept knoll

1891, noted that Christmas was observed at Oro Blanco with a highly successful entertainment and ball that were a "credit to the place." There were "fully" 100 people present.

"This was the largest congregation of people from Yellow Jacket, Arivaca, Warsaw and other neighboring camps that has ever taken place here," the article said.

"There has been many a horse race on the street that ran in front of the old adobe buildings on Dia San Juan (June 24). In early days, the Mexicans had a fiesta and horseracing there on that holiday," Noon added.

"The school house where my mother taught was also the center for dances and parties," he said.

Oro Blanco, wreathed in its aura of the past, is a good place for remembering.

PARADISE
the 'jail tree' survives

For the adventuresome with a desire to go to Paradise, there is a way.

Paradise, in this instance, is not an intangible somewhere in the morrow. It is a quiet shadow of its once booming self, snuggled in the recesses of the Chiricahua Mountains in southeastern Arizona.

Paradise, in a trip there in February, was in the icy grip of winter. Turkey Creek trickled with melting snow. Bluejays chattered among the pinon pines, scrub oaks and junipers.

Slithering like a snake through the hills, Turkey Creek Drive is also the "main street." Along its path are remains of an old post office, old houses and assorted crumbling foundations.

The jail tree, a sturdy black oak, seemed wreathed in memories of the prisoners once handcuffed to its girth. And, near the end of the quiet land stood a weatherbeaten house, the home of W. W. Sanders, a first-rate narrator. Sanders came to Paradise with his parents in 1902.

It was in 1903, Sanders said, (some say 1901) that a Michigan copper mining company, the Chiricahua Development Co., sank a double compartment shaft 480 feet. Although the shaft ran in two big drifts and nearly a half million dollars were sunk in the mine, the company's expectations were not met. The firm moved to Superior in 1905, Sanders said.

In boom days there were 18 houses, tents, a few stores, a hotel and an ample supply of saloons in Paradise.

"There were the Old Owl, the Cockatoo, and the Meadow Park Saloons," he said. "Charlie Randolph, a saloon owner, was the first man to die in Paradise. Getting into saloon operations was easy. If a man could get hold of $10, he could buy a barrel of whiskey for $5. If he made good, he was in business."

Violence? Sanders considered the question. "One man was murdered in the Old Owl. The victim had bragged he was going to shoot a deputy the next day, and one of the Powers boys shot him.

"There was a holdup one night," Sanders continued. "A fellow by the name of Slivers, a gambler, had won $3,000 in a saloon, and it was a known fact that he had hit it pretty good.

"Two fellows held him up on the dark side of a hill when he went home. They searched all over him, but found no money. Slivers was too clever. He had hid the money in the crown of his hat. He also recognized one of his assailants as one of the 'law and order' men."

Sanders said the mail came in by stage coach and a team of four

W. W. Sanders at home in Paradise

horses. Later, a car replaced the horse-drawn vehicle. The post office established in 1901 was discontinued in 1943.

Pointing to a green cottage, Sanders said, "Grandpa Walker, father of George Walker, the first businessman here, built that house when he was 81. He planted three apple trees, and people said he'd never live to eat the fruit. But he did."

There are at least two versions of how the mining camp got its name. Some say miners gave the town its exotic name. The men who traveled to San Simon for supplies were scorched by the summer heat. Back in camp, they took a drink of cool spring water, and sighed, "Yep, this is Paradise."

Sanders said that Walker, who laid out the townsite, named the town. Walker brought his bride to the settlement on their honeymoon and because of their happiness named the place Paradise.

Sanders also recalled a jailbreak.

"The jail tree had been replaced by a limestone jail," said the pioneer, drawing another tale from his store of memories. "A Mexican prisoner escaped by digging beneath the walls. He was lassoed and brought back to Paradise, but not to the new jail. He was tied to the security of the black oak."

(In 1977, there were an estimated five families living permanently in the quiet historical place.)

PEARCE
scene of gold rush

Commonwealth Hill, gouged of millions of dollars in gold, basked stolidly in the noontide sun when Robert E. Crouch of Glendale made a sentimental journey to this pioneer community of his boyhood.

He tilted his broad-brimmed hat and scanned Main Street, a wraith-like shadow of the once bustling community. The collection of buildings was hard to equate with his memories.

Adobe houses melted in the weather and time, their windows and doorways gaping meaninglessly. The jail house and old post office lay idle. The store, built in 1893, was a lively remnant.

William D. Monmonier, justice of peace here during Pearce's livelier days, was Crouch's grandfather. That house, with parlor walls once lined with the Judge's lawbooks, was a decaying specter. Its creaking timbers and festoons of wallpaper rustled in the wind. It was hard to believe that the old house was once the seat of justice.

The town got its start in 1894 when John James Pearce, a rancher and prospector, was scouting the area and stopped on Commonwealth Hill for a bite of lunch. Afterwards he cracked a piece of dark heavy outcrop and jumped in excitement. The specimen showed free gold.

Pearce, for whom the town was named, filed several claims. Some

say, when the word of discovery hit, Tombstone was almost depopulated. Some people walked in with packs on their backs, hurrying to the new gold field.

The town flourished. Pearce sold out for $250,000. Peak production probably came in 1896. Still later there was a mine cave-in. Some sources say inrushing water started the mine's doom. It closed in 1918, but operated sporadically until about 1930. Store owner Bob Seaton said five families lived here in 1969.

"Things may break loose again one of these days," Seaton said. "Core drilling for gold, silver and copper in the area may put Pearce back on the map."

Seaton, a lapidary fan and retired telephone employee, said that thousands last year visited his quaint store, which contains a little shrine museum devoted to Abraham Lincoln.

Forgotten happenings began surfacing as Crouch walked main street, then veered by the old school house, alongside its more modern counterpart. "I began my schooling there," he said. "That's where on Halloween night a boy locked up some goats inside and they ate up the textbooks."

Long ago, the children of Pearce invented their own entertainment. One sport was chasing mockingbirds on burro back.

"We caged them for pets," said Crouch. "Sometimes they sang out

at midnight."

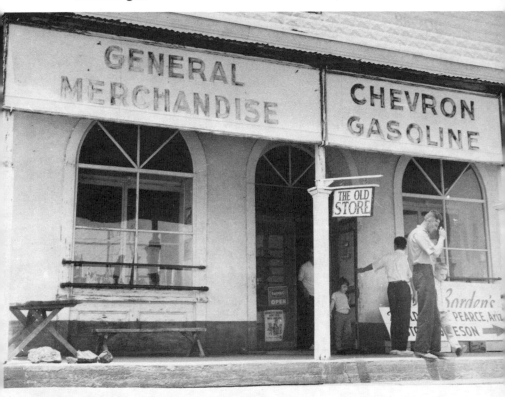

SASCO
acronym of the past

Certainly, any greatness this town possessed lies in its past. The evidence so speaks.

The town is dead. It's even doubtful there are any ghosts still hanging around.

A lizard slithered across the cement floor of a once sizable house, and somewhere in the distance, a bird called from a palo verde treetop. The scent of sagebrush was heady.

The railroad that brought in ore for smelting from the Silver Bell Mine and transport on to Red Rock is gone. So is the old mill and the town's total population.

But, the haunting vibes are good. There are more remnants than usually found in ghost towns.

Adventurers with a taste for history savor such places. So it was that a quartet swung off I-10 at Red Rock and motored west for Sasco, about seven miles away.

Picnic baskets, cameras, broad-brimmed hats and thermos jugs were packed in standby readiness as the car nosed ahead. For a time, the course was on a paved road marked "dangerous but passable." Then came the rutted dirt road, forking at least once, and twice crossed with water.

The desert trail snaked through brush and mesquite areas and ahead the mountains were purple cast. Suddenly, there loomed a roofless rock building, possibly a rooming house during Sasco's

Remains of rooming house gape in emptiness at Sasco.

heyday:

Sasco—an acronym for Southern Arizona Smelting Co.—was founded in the early 1900s. By 1904 the Arizona Southern Railroad was in, and by 1907 a post office was established here. During lively times, several hundred people lived here.

Historians note there were stores, lodging, saloons. And, as could

Smelter furnace relic at Sasco

be expected, at least one murder was committed in the town.

The smelter furnace was closed due to insufficient profits, records relate, and in 1919 the post office shut down. The railroad and smelter later were torn down for junk.

The trail beyond the rock building beckoned and ahead, still clinging to the mountain, was part of the old smelter furnace. Nearby were other parts of the mill.

After lunch in the stillness of the mountains and without a single other visitor, there were more areas to explore. There were foundations, some with basements. A huge rock fountain that no longer gushed with water whetted the imagination. Perhaps it once was in the center of the town plaza.

Not far away were other adobe walls in interesting shapes and sizes.

Sasco offers one departure from the usual ghost town. Still discernible is a sign on a concrete structure which faintly proclaims "City Hall." Maybe that, too, is a figment of someone's imagination!

SUNNYSIDE
"the Salvation Army camp"

Communal living once flourished at Sunnyside, Arizona, now a ghost town in the remote, wooded section of the Huachuca Mountains.

John McIntyre, 76, still a hardy remnant of that long ago religious community, returned to live at Sunnyside, scene of his early boyhood.

It's quiet and peaceful on top of Music Hill, where McIntyre has built a modern home. The vantage point overlooks the time-eroded Sunnyside buildings.

Deer venture close enough for McIntyre and his wife, Anna, to watch from their many windowed home.

The walnut tree saplings, where McIntyre swung as a fun loving boy, are old and gnarled. A tree stump bespeaks of the dinner gong, which once swung from the limb of a juniper tree to summon residents to the communal dining hall.

Sunnyside has a history unique among Arizona ghost towns, its very beginning setting it apart from other once hell-raising towns. There are no remains of bars nor hanging trees. Sunnyside's history records no murders nor crimes of passion. Singularly, it was founded for religious reasons.

Sunnyside began in the late 1880s, McIntyre said, by the leadership of the Scotch born Samuel Donnelly, a former sailor and prize fighter, converted one night at a Salvation Army meeting in San Francisco. He later founded the inter-denominational community of "Bible-gleaning Christians," and the settlement was sometimes referred to as the "Salvation Army Camp."

McIntyre pointed to the exact spot of his desk in the crumbling school house. Even the old blackboard remains. Young John attended the one room school in 1903. His Alabama born school teacher started the day's teaching of the 3Rs with a Bible verse or good quotation.

The former pupil recited one: "Truth crushed will rise again."

The pioneer remembered that the 50 families earned their living by operating a community saw mill, cutting hay on contract for Fort Huachuca, using their draft horses for railroad grading, or working in nearby mines. But, regardless of where they worked, residents funneled their money into a common treasury.

And, the man who would eat but not work was ordered out.

There were no stores in the town and the homes contained no kitchens, for everyone ate at the community dining hall. Food was

John McIntyre at threshold of school he attended in 1903

hauled in by wagon from Fairbank or Tombstone to Garden Canyon, where burros took the burden to Sunnyside.

Women divided the cooking chores at the huge army range. Some were bakers, pastry cooks and dishwashers. Others were seamstresses.

Once a year, on the Fourth of July, the community, specially the children, enjoyed an ice cream treat. Ice was wrapped in canvas and brought in by burros from Ft. Huachuca.

"One year a storm came up and no ice could be brought in," McIntyre, a devout man, recalled. "We were awfully disappointed. But, then the Lord sent a good hail and we had ice cream after all."

A few years ago McIntyre knocked down the tumbling 24 x 18 foot dining hall. But, he marked with a boulder the spot of the head table from which prayers of thanksgiving were raised before mealtime.

Another shack marks the community laundry, still with a bin where soiled clothes were dumped to be washed cooperatively once a week in a homemade washing machine. Soft soap, also homemade, was used.

A screened room with layers of shelving remains of the milk room, where pans of milk cooled for the hungry clan.

Even death brought community effort, with the men making the casket of juniper planks. The crude coffin was then cloth-lined with care by the womenfolk.

In time, with the closing of area mines and the resulting abandonment of the saw mill, residents moved on in separate ways. But, apparently, communal living did work for the religious camp.

"People visiting the community would remark how happy the people seemed," Mrs. McIntyre reported. "They had food and raiment and were content."

McIntyre, whose father was a merchant in Dodge City, Kansas, came first to southern Arizona with his family to the Copper Glance Mining Camp in 1893. His father later taught school in Sunnyside. Then the family moved on to historic Tombstone.

Sunnyside, now privately owned with McIntyre's nephew, the administrator, is reached by a rough trail about 40 miles northwest of Bisbee.

McIntyre described Donnelly, who died in 1901, as a "spirit-filled man. Although he was not formally educated, people who heard him knew the Lord was his teacher."

Sunnyside residents in early days often went to church in the Lone Star Camp, three miles away. A big event occured in Sunnyside when the music teacher had a piano brought in around the mountains by a team of horses to her home on top a hill.

That's why the knoll overlooking the camp was called "Music Hill."

TOTAL WRECK
a short, happy life

Only some time-worn remnants remain, a meager legacy of what was once a thriving silver mining community here.

Hidden in the Empire Mountains, Total Wreck is a tough place to find—and the name of this ghost town still intrigues history buffs.

A previous attempt to find it years ago failed.

But last spring, this writer and three others, armed with better directions, cameras, binoculars and ample food, water and gas resumed the quest.

We turned south of Interstate 10 about 24 miles east of Tucson and were peering out the four-wheel drive vehicles as it nosed down and then up one gully after another on a desert trail.

Total Wreck, historians note, was discovered by chance in 1879 by miners John T. Dillon and his boss, Walter Vail. Dillon pointed to several granite and quartz formations on an eastern slope of the Empires. He declared the hill "looked like a total wreck."

Desert vegetation this time of the year was interesting. There were carmine tipped ocotillos and flowers. Occasionally, the car was at eye-level with buster-sized purple thistles, worked by yellow and black bees.

Windmills dotted the landscape and often the road parallelled a high-pressure gas line. But over-riding the feelings sparked by the scenic beauty was a sense of anticipation. Was this the right road or would our quest end dismally on the wrong route again?

A sense of adventure melded with anxiety. There also was the knowledge that Total Wreck would be but a forlorn fragment when, and if, found.

"If we're on the right trail, Total Wreck must be near," someone conjectured hopefully. "Let's go another mile or so."

We had been on the trail about 45 minutes, traveling slowly due to the rough terrain and occasional stops for a quick picture or two. The trail veered into the mountains and we rounded a bend to find a rewarding sight. Looking like a wraith of the past, two boulder walls, apparently part of the old mill, clutched to the mountainside.

The vehicle halted. Everyone bailed out for a closer look.

Our explorations were marked by caution as more than one open mine was noted. Batches of rotted lumber gave the place a truly total wreck look.

Driving beyond the camp, the trail became steep and there was need for four-wheel drive power.

Around a bend in the trail, a quartet of visitors entering from a

different road reported they encountered a hostile landowner. There was even a report that a man had been shot at—certainly food for thought.

Back at the mill, the scene was quiet and serene. A squirrel dashed by and Indian wheat grass bowed in the breeze. A huge concrete pillar served as table for picnic fare.

It was a good time to reflect on Total Wreck's past.

Back in 1879, Vail, Dillon and another man found on closer inspection that the rock formations appeared to bare traces of silver. The men posted locations on three sites, calling one Total Wreck. Preliminary tests on the Total Wreck mine revealed 40 ounces silver to a ton of ore.

From that chance discovery, the Total Wreck Mining and Milling Co. was formed in 1881, with brothers Nathan and Walter Vail the principal shareholders.

The Vails dared to innovate and invest. As the mine sank deeper and deeper, they added a mill and hoisting works, a 600-foot tramway from the mine to the mill, a massive steam-powered hoist above the mine shaft, and a one-ton ore car to travel from the surface to underground mine levels.

Water was brought in from a creek two miles south and two 50,000 gallon redwood tanks in the town provided ample water for the mill and its residents.

When the mine was in full operation, area newspapers hailed it as second to none in the West.

As the mine succeeded, Total Wreck thrived. In 1883, 50 houses, three hotels, a brewery, four saloons, a bunkhouse, bank and lumberyard dotted its streets. The butcher shop featured beef from the Empire Ranch. The town's population of 300 bulged when miners throughout the area came to Total Wreck to trade, drink and gamble.

But Edward Vail, mine assayer, labeled Total Wreck an orderly town despite the goings-on there.

"To my knowledge no one was killed in a gunfight, but there were some close calls," he was quoted as saying.

George P. Dowell told the Arizona Historical Society at its recent convention the mill at one time was processing between 65 and 70 tons of ore daily.

But like bonanza towns, there came a day when diminishing mine yields combined with the depression in silver prices to cripple the mining camp.

Eventually mining operations came to a standstill, and in 1890 the government ceased operation of the post office. The population drifted away, most miners dismantling their homes and moving to thriving Arizona copper towns.

Total Wreck's life was lively but limited.

GRAVEYARDS
monuments to man's mortality

A small cemetery clutching a hillside in the Harshaw mining camp ghost town area in Santa Cruz County must be one of the most unusual in the state.

But, in another little cemetery near Red Rock and ghost town Sasco, a burial place depicts remembrances of long ago residents in different variations. One grave is marked by a bedstead headboard —front and foot.

And, in a forgotten recess of old Goldroad in Mohave County some graves are surrounded by individual picket fences, many now bowing to age.

Many, many mining camps had cemeteries. Part and parcel of the Old West, the graveyards—in a way—reflect the life and times of the mining camp era.

The Harshaw area burial grounds is a case in point. Many markers are improvised. They are as varied as the taste, pocketbook and sentiment of loved ones left behind.

Miniature shrines in concrete are perched above some graves. There are granite headstones, obviously put there long after the deaths that date back as far as 1885.

Others are simple wooden crosses with crucifix. Some crosses are of iron pipe with doorknobs at the end for ornaments. There is even

John Lynch examines styrofoam cross at Harshaw Cemetery.

Line of headstones in isolated cemetery at Harshaw

a cross made of inverted styrofoam egg cartons.

And throughout, there are plastic flowers that despite fading are evidence of those who still care.

Then there are the old and apparently forgotten burial plots ravaged by time. They are simply outlined by rocks and bear undecipherable markers—or none at all.

The mining camp in the area was named for David T. Harshaw, a prominent citizen who came to the place originally called Durasno, in 1873.

In the Sorrels' family plot encircled with a stone fence are three granite tombstones, one indicating the most recent death in 1907.

The epitaphs are novel.

One for a child says simply, "A little time on earth he spent, yet God for him his angel sent."

The tombstone for Ahera Sorrels bore this more lengthy inscription:

"What to us is life without thee? Darkness and despair alone. When with sighs we seek to find thee, this tomb proclaims that you are gone."

*Fancy fencing
and
plastic flowers
embellish
grave at Sasco.*

*Bedstead
headboards
mark grave
near Sasco.*

INDEX

Dates in parentheses identify the author's most recent visit.

ORDER BLANK

GOLDEN WEST PUBLISHERS

☼ 4113 N. Longview Ave. • Phoenix, AZ 85014

www.goldenwestpublishers.com • **1-800-658-5830** • FAX 602-279-6901

Qty	Title	Price	Amount
	Arizona Cook Book	5.95	
	Arizona Trivia	8.95	
	Discover Arizona!	6.95	
	Explore Arizona!	6.95	
	Fishing Arizona	9.95	
	Ghost Towns in Arizona	6.95	
	Haunted Highway—The Spirits of Route 66	12.95	
	Hiking Arizona	6.95	
	Hiking Arizona II	6.95	
	Hiking Central Arizona	5.95	
	Hiking Northern Arizona	5.95	
	Horse Trails in Arizona	12.95	
	In Old Arizona	6.95	
	Kokopelli's Cook Book	9.95	
	Motorcycle Arizona	9.95	
	Quest for the Dutchman's Gold	6.95	
	Scorpions & Venomous Insects of the SW	9.95	
	Sedona Cook Book	7.95	
	Snakes and other Reptiles of the SW	9.95	
	Verde River Recreation Guide	9.95	
Shipping & Handling Add ⫸	U.S. & Canada	$3.00	
	Other countries	$5.00	

☐ My Check or Money Order Enclosed $

☐ MasterCard ☐ VISA ($20 credit card minimum)

(Payable in U.S. funds)

Acct. No.	Exp. Date
Signature	
Name	Telephone
Address	
City/State/Zip 2/00	**Call for FREE catalog** Ghost Towns

This order blank may be photo-copied.